Creating the AHRC

British Academy Occasional Paper, 12

British Academy Occasional Papers are a series of paperback volumes on topics of current interest.

The British Academy, established by Royal Charter in 1902, is the national academy for the humanities and the social sciences. It is an independent, self-governing fellowship of more than 800 scholars, elected for distinction and achievement in one or more branches of the academic disciplines that make up the humanities and social sciences.

The British Academy supports postdoctoral research in the humanities and social sciences through its research grants schemes, promoting relations between researchers in the UK and overseas, and recognising distinction in scholarship. It runs a varied programme of events, and has an active publications programme. It also engages with and advises on major policy issues in the higher education sector.

Creating the AHRC

An Arts and Humanities Research Council
for the United Kingdom
in the Twenty-first Century

JAMES HERBERT

Published for THE BRITISH ACADEMY

by OXFORD UNIVERSITY PRESS

2008

Oxford University Press, Great Clarendon Street, Oxford OX2 6DP

Oxford New York
Auckland Cape Town Dar es Salaam Hong Kong Karachi
Kuala Lumpur Madrid Melbourne Mexico City Nairobi
New Delhi Shanghai Taipei Toronto

With offices in
Argentina Austria Brazil Chile Czech Republic France Greece
Guatemala Hungary Italy Japan Poland Portugal Singapore
South Korea Switzerland Thailand Turkey Ukraine Vietnam

Published in the United States
by Oxford University Press Inc., New York

© The British Academy 2008
Database right The British Academy (maker)
First published 2008

British Library Cataloguing in Publication Data
Data available

Library of Congress Cataloging in Publication Data
Data available

Typeset in the offices of the British Academy
Printed in Great Britain
on acid-free paper by
CPI Antony Rowe, Chippenham, Wiltshire

ISBN 978-0-19-726429-4

Contents

Illustrations

Preface

Readers of this account will include, I hope, the many people who will have the opportunity and pleasure of working with the Arts and Humanities Research Council in the coming years. It is worth realizing how the AHRC came to be the special organization it is. As the notes in the following volume indicate, the creators of the AHRC were no less constructive and generous in communicating with me than they were in founding the organization itself. Brian Follett and Frances Marsden provided unfailing encouragement. The AHRC itself helped defray the expenses of several trips from Cambridge to London and Bristol. The Centre for Research in the Arts, Social Sciences and Humanities of the University of Cambridge provided an incomparable academic home, beginning with a Visiting Fellowship in Michaelmas Term 2005 and continuing in the 2006-2007 academic year. Ludmilla Jordanova and Mary Jacobus, successive Directors of the Centre, were warm and thoughtful hosts. The timely assistance of Malcolm Bowie, Master of Christ's College, holds a permanent place in my memory. Deft work by James Rivington of the British Academy and Molly Conisbee of the Arts and Humanities Research Council brought this volume into being. It is dedicated to my wife, Sandra Herbert, without whom I may not have ventured across the Atlantic.

A · H · R · B

arts and humanities research board

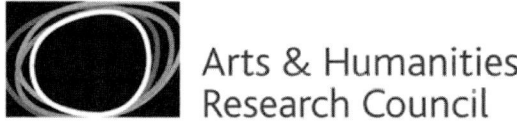 Arts & Humanities
Research Council

The AHRB logo was designed in the British Academy's Publications Department.
The AHRC logo was designed by VHD, Bristol.

I

A False Start

Most modern governments reinvest a small part of national income in the generation of new knowledge. In the United Kingdom the Department for Scientific and Industrial Research carried out this function until 1965. Then the Science and Technology Act shifted responsibility for curiosity-driven research to five Research Councils, funded through the Department of Education and Science. In 1993 a widely influential White Paper, *Realizing Our Potential,* heralded reorganization of the Research Councils under an Office of Science and Technology, which was placed in the Cabinet Office under the leadership of William Waldegrave. Within the Office of Science and Technology a new civil service post was created: director-general of Research Councils. The overall theme of *Realizing Our Potential* was how science might better contribute to wealth creation and the quality of life in the United Kingdom.[1]

While the 1965 legislation had not created a Research Council for the humanities, the possibility had been suggested. A 1961 review by the British Academy had recommended, 'We should therefore like to see established a Council for Research in the Humanities and the Social Sciences.'[2] Ultimately this recommendation found a double-edged response, reported by the then Secretary of the Academy. 'Our report had been studied and its main contentions were accepted.' Still, while 'provision for the Social Sciences was already under consideration in another context,' there was no need to create an independent central body for the distribution of funds in the humanities. 'The work could be done equally well by the British Academy itself.' The only reservation was that for the purpose of making grants the Academy 'should adhere solely to the pure

"Humanities".'[3] A separate Research Council for the social sciences was, in fact, established in 1965.

Discussion in the early 1990s of reorganizing UK research funding reopened the question of how the government supported research in the humanities.[4] The role of the British Academy had grown considerably. In 1962 the Academy could announce that the Treasury had agreed to an annual grant of £25,000 to support research in humanistic studies; by 1969 that grant stood at £65,000. In 1976 the Academy agreed to administer a scheme of 'small grants in the humanities' that, by the following year, made awards totalling £215,000. As of 1984 the Academy was also administering an approximately £10 million programme of postgraduate studentships for the Department of Education and Science.[5] Thus, by the early 1990s, the British Academy had good reason to join public deliberation concerning the future of research funding, particularly as it had to do with the humanities. The Academy convened three separate study groups whose reports were published in June 1990, June 1991, and December 1991.

The four-member 1990 working party included Anthony Kenny, President of the British Academy and Keith Thomas, a future President of the Academy.[6] Its report was presented to and endorsed by the Council of the Academy on 29 June. The report was organized so as to present alternative funding arrangements as well as arguments both for and against any new course of action. The options included: a freestanding Humanities Research Council; a new Humanities and Social Science Research Council; some kind of new council with the British Academy retaining some government support and grant-making functions (like the Royal Society); a separate Research Council wing organized within the Academy; and the Academy itself becoming a Research Council.

The arguments for a Humanities Research Council revolved around what the Working Party called the 'muffled voice of the humanities'. Recent government decisions had led to reducing the number of postgraduate studentships in the humanities as well as to stipends lower than in fields with Research Councils. 'The Academy, accordingly, had to bear the odium for a situation in which graduate students in the humanities were uniquely discriminated against.'[7] Furthermore, not only were the humanities underfunded in proportion to their share of the academic workforce, but also new higher education funding arrangements—being discussed without humanities participation—threatened to increase humanities teachers' workload and reduce support for the libraries they relied on. The arguments against a Humanities Research Council came down to just two. Since the British Academy operated largely on a volunteer basis, setting up a Research Council would require public money that could be better spent elsewhere. Secondly, a government-appointed Research Council 'could include lay members who might need educating about the intrinsic value of the humanities.' Such a body might favour group over individual research or politicize controversial issues.[8]

The 1990 report considered several ways of working with a social science council but finally concluded: 'If there is to be a new Research Council with responsibility for the humanities, the Working Party would prefer it to be a newly constituted Research Council for the Humanities alone.'[9] It recommended that such a council be set up, 'provided certain conditions were met.' The appointment process for the Council should ensure that it be sufficiently aware of the differences between research in the humanities and research in the natural or social sciences. The Council should be adequately funded. And third, transfer of funding away from the British Academy should leave the Academy, like the Royal Society, with some responsibility for disbursement of public funds.[10]

By December 1991, the Academy reported in a rather more urgent tone that its Council was giving serious consideration to the advantages and disadvantages of a joint Humanities and Social Science Research Council. It had agreed with the Economic and

Social Research Council (ESRC) to set up 'a joint working party to explore the detailed practicality of such a proposal' although that exploration was not to prejudice the Academy's 'clear first preference'.[11]

The ten-member joint working party, chaired by Brian Follett, Biological Secretary of the Royal Society, took a broader perspective. It spelled out a clear and uncluttered case for a public agency to fund humanities research. It straightforwardly compared the fashioning of a single 'Humanities, Economic and Social Research Council' (HESRC) to establishing a 'Humanities Research Council' (HRC) alongside the existing ESRC and the other Research Councils. It concluded that an HESRC was technically feasible, but that it would save little in administrative costs and disrupt the only recently recovered equilibrium of the ESRC. Having reviewed carefully the 'intellectual, representational, financial, and administrative' arguments, the joint working party 'strongly' recommended establishing a Humanities Research Council. Its report became available in September 1992, five months after an April election had returned the Conservative Government to power.[12]

A period of decision-making followed closely on the 1992 election. Waldegrave was appointed to the Cabinet Office and the Office of Science and Technology (OST) was set up. The following February the House of Lords conducted a full-scale debate concerning creation of a Humanities Research Council. On 20 May 1993 the Department for Education's Parliamentary Under-Secretary of State, Timothy Boswell met with British Academy representatives Anthony Kenny and Peter W. H. Brown, Secretary of the Academy. Boswell conveyed the Government's decision not to set up an agency to support humanities research, emphasizing that it was not just a departmental decision, but a collective Governmental one, based on the merits of the case.[13] Six days later, on 26 May 1993, *Realizing Our Potential* was published.

The Government's 1993 decision not to admit the humanities in any form to the circle of Research Councils disappointed many humanities scholars and members of the British Academy. Some of the latter even argued against continuing to administer postgraduate studentships and other research programmes funded by the Government.[14] Eventually a compromise option was adopted. In 1994 the Academy set up a separate Humanities Research Board (HRB) to administer most of the government-financed programmes.[15] The HRB's first Chairman was Professor John Laver, a prominent linguistics scholar and Vice-Principal for Research and Postgraduate Studies at the University of Edinburgh. Dr Michael Jubb of the Academy staff took on responsibility for day-to-day administration of the HRB. The greater number of HRB members were from outside the British Academy. In 1995 the new HRB was receiving £16.7 million from the by-then Department of Education and Employment for its postgraduate and other humanities research awards.[16] Also, toward the end of 1995, the Government surprised and chagrined many scientists by making the Office of Science and Technology part of the Department of Trade and Industry.[17]

NOTES

[1] Tom Wilke, 'Science' in Dennis Kavanagh and Anthony Seldon (eds.) *The Major Effect* (London: Macmillan, 1994), pp. 433-443. The reorganized research councils were: the Medical Research Council (MRC); the Engineering and Physical Sciences Research Council (EPSRC); the Particle Physics and Astronomy Research Council (PPARC); the Biotechnology and Biological Sciences Research Council (BBSRC); and the Economic and Social Research Council (ESRC).

[2] *Research in the Humanities and the Social Sciences: Report of a Survey by the British Academy 1958-1960* (Oxford University Press for the British Academy, London, 1961), p. 71. Established by Royal Charter in 1902, the British Academy received its first annual grant from the Government in 1924: £2000 for promotion of research and publication. By 1950 the annual grant was £5000.

3 Mortimer Wheeler, *The British Academy 1949-1968* (Oxford University Press for the British Academy, London, 1970), p. 47. Wheeler was Secretary of the British Academy at the time; Henry Brooke, Financial Secretary of the Treasury, gave the response.

4 Such discussion seemed to begin as John Major became Prime Minister in 1990. Between 1985 and 1992 UK investment in research and development declined from 2.25% to 2.12% of GDP. The UK was scheduled to become President of the European Community in 1992, and many considered the representation in Brussels of British science and technology weak and divided. Wilke, pp. 431-441. Moreover, in 1991 the government erased the distinction between universities and polytechnics and removed further education colleges from local control. Thus the Department of Education and Science had to adjust focus to include many institutions of higher education whose primary mission was not scientific research. Peter Scott, 'Education Policy' in Kavanagh and Seldon, p. 338. Under these circumstances the CVCP [Committee of Vice Chancellors and Principals, predecessor of today's Universities UK] stressed the importance of the 'dual funding system' under which research projects and postgraduate studentships were funded through the Research Councils (which as yet did not include the humanities). *Arcady* No. 2 (Spring 2000), p. 1.

5 *The British Academy 1902-2002: Some Historical Documents and Notes* (British Academy, 2002), pp. 22-26. [hereafter '*BA Some Documents*']

6 Kenny, a philosopher, was then a Fellow of St. John's College, Oxford and Warden of Rhodes House, Oxford. Thomas, an historian, was then President of Corpus Christi College, Oxford. The other members were M.A. Boden, then Professor of Philosophy and Psychology, University of Sussex and Peter Mathias, an economic historian, then Master of Downing College, Cambridge.

7 The British Academy, *Report of a Working Party on a Humanities Research Council* (June 1990), p. 12. [hereafter '*Report of a Working Party*']

8 *Report of a Working Party*, p. 15.

9 *Report of a Working Party*, p. 16.

10 *Report of a Working Party*, pp. 16-17.

11 The British Academy, *A Research Council for the Humanities*, 11 December 1991, [p. 4]. One source of urgency may have been the Government. Peter Brown, personal communication, 5 October 2007.

12 *The Future of Research Funding in the Humanities and Social Sciences: Report of a Joint Working Party Established by the British Academy and the Economic and Social Research Council* [undated], especially pp. 9, 11. [The report was available by September 1992 according to: Brian Follett, personal communication, 6 July 2007.]

13 Peter Brown, personal communication, 6 December 2007.

[14] Michael Jubb, personal communication, 16 March 2007.

[15] The Academy itself continued to administer support for some research positions and for small research and conference grants in the social sciences. The HRB assumed responsibility for postgraduate studentships, research leave, and major research, small research and conference grants in the humanities. *BA Some Documents*, p.29.

[16] *The Times Higher Education Supplement,* 8 September 1995. [hereafter 'THES']. British Academy, *Annual Report 1993-95*. Cf. Chapter II, Note 26.

[17] THES 29 December 1995.

II

Back on to the Agenda

In recent years policy scholars have devoted much thought to formation of the public agenda. Many point out that public attention is a scarce commodity and show how getting it involves competing in the relevant arenas. Among the huge number of possible issues, only a few become the focus of public concern. Small communities of professionals, interest groups, and activists keep other issues alive. One distinction between the 'policy stream' and the 'problem stream' helps explain how such other issues stay afloat. The policy stream flows along, carrying 'solutions waiting for problems'. Ongoing discussion of possible courses of public action refines them and makes them familiar, in what one scholar calls the 'diminishing astonishment principle'. Problems, however, bubble up less predictably, and only briefly claim public attention. Policy responses must be found near at hand. One text calls effective political advocates 'matchmakers' and 'brokers of problems with solutions'.[1] The issue of a Research Council for the humanities came into the mainstream of public, and governmental, attention when it was fastened to the problem of financing higher education, which itself was tied to fears about the future of the UK economy, given a decline in traditional manufacturing.

In May of 1996 the Secretary of State for Education and Employment together with the Secretaries of State for Wales, Scotland and Northern Ireland appointed — 'with bipartisan support', Chairman Ron Dearing was careful to tell us — a seventeen-member 'National Committee of Inquiry into Higher Education'. In May of 1997, a national election set the stage for a new public agenda. Shortly thereafter, in July 1997, the National Committee published its report: *Higher Education in a Learning Society*. It came to be called the

Dearing Report (in fact, there have been at least three).[2] In charting a course for higher education in the UK for the next twenty years, this massive study developed what might be called an 'intellectual capital' approach. The well-being and especially the prosperity of the 'learning society' will require increasing numbers of highly educated people. Enrolment caps should be discarded, the quality of teaching and learning should be made more attractive, and students should participate in the financing of what will be their increasingly valuable educations. Further, the growing need for research had overburdened existing university facilities and equipment. Fuller investment in the research infrastructure would make UK researchers more productive. The ten volumes of the Dearing Report elaborated this 'intellectual capital' analysis in a Summary Report, the Main Report, five appendices and fourteen special reports. It offered 93 specific recommendations.[3] Chapter 11 of the Main Report was entitled 'Supporting research and scholarship' and there, together with eight other recommendations, was Recommendation 29:

> We recommend to the Government that a new Arts and Humanities Research Council (AHRC) should be established as soon as possible.[4]

Behind this unequivocal, straightforward recommendation lay a paper prepared by Professor John Laver of the University of Edinburgh. At the time Laver was, as we have noted, Chairman of the British Academy's Humanities Research Board. Aptly entitled 'The need to invest in research in the humanities and the arts', Laver's paper eventually appeared as Appendix 3 of the Dearing Report. Laver was careful to acknowledge the familiar 'intrinsic benefits' of the humanities: 'an enhanced quality of mind, and … the ability … to participate in, and contribute constructively to, a rational and culturally rich society'.[5] Likewise he noted that, 'while the linkage of science to wealth creation is usually direct, the economic impact of research in the humanities and the arts, while very substantial, is typically more indirect.'[6] Nonetheless, fresh, exciting, and pivotal sections of Laver's paper called attention to various 'instrumental' or economic benefits of the humanities. Such benefits pervade virtually every sector of society: the publishing industry, the tourism and leisure industry, diplomacy, international trade, and the major export business of education and training. Laver noted that the last, education for export, was a £7 billion industry in the UK, growing by 15% a year. He added that 18% of the UK's foreign full-time postgraduate students were in the humanities.[7]

Many of the 'instrumental benefits' cited by Laver had to do with language, the very neural system of the humanities. The paper recalled that English is an official language in 70 countries with a population of 1.4 billion and that it has important status in 20 other countries. One out of five human beings speaks English and many of the others wish to learn it. Humanities graduates, Laver observed, train the 500,000 foreign students who travel to Britain each year to study English.[8] With respect to other languages, he reported that a converging Europe already employed 190,000 translators. While the European Community needed to translate one million pages of documents in a single year, the information age brought even greater challenges. Localizing software designed in one language into all the languages of Europe, for example, required 50% of the overall cost of development.[9]

Against this background, Laver argued that the 'marginalization of humanities research is a waste of national talent.' He reported that an average of less than £950 a year was available to support the work of a research-active member of the humanities staff in a UK university.[10] Laver pointed out that the resulting sole-practitioner 'straightjacket of research funding' prevented humanities scholars from benefiting from research-accelerating and cost-effective assistance, and from engaging in adequately supported interdisciplinary collaborative research.[11] As a result, 'it is clear that new knowledge in the humanities is being gathered at a much slower rate than in the sciences.'[12] Given the National Committee's emphasis on the importance of intellectual capital, this delay sounded like part of the problem.

Directing attention to the place of the humanities (and the arts) among the other disciplines, the National Committee took up Laver's argument. Its section on the arts and humanities began:

> The arts and humanities do not have a Research Council, which puts them at a disadvantage as they do not have direct involvement in high level discussion about research funding and policy. Given the substantial contribution they make to the social and economic prosperity of the nation, we considered a number of options to ensure that research in the arts and humanities is adequately supported.[13]

Indeed, the Committee suggested that the humanities would respond even more to increasing investment than some other fields: 'technological advances ... will have proportionately greater influence in subjects that depend on library access and on bodies of data, than in some of the sciences.'[14]

The 'learning society' foreseen by the National Committee required more careful attention to both teaching and research. Its report recounted strong testimony that 'the [Higher Education] Funding Bodies' procedures reward institutions for excellence in research and not teaching which leads individuals, departments, and institutions to focus on research activity to the detriment of teaching.' The Committee resolved that its proposals for funding research would, as far as possible, 'promote not devalue teaching.'[15]

Funding Councils support university teaching and research through separate streams of money. Their role with respect to research, however, focuses on institutional infrastructure. 'One of the key purposes of the allocation from the Funding Bodies is to contribute to the costs of infrastructure of projects funded by sponsors such as the Research Councils...' Such support for institutional infrastructure is distributed retrospectively, by means of the well-known and less-liked Research Assessment Exercise (RAE). But it was the job of the Research Councils to identify and invest 'prospectively' in specific, promising research projects.[16] Thus the Dearing Report strongly endorsed the 'dual support' approach to funding research: retrospective Funding Council support to institutions of higher education, complemented by prospective Research Council support for specific research projects. This endorsement threw into bold relief that there was no such Research Council for the arts and humanities.

The suddenly prominent place of the arts in the Dearing Report deserves explicit notice. John Laver's paper, written earlier than the Main Report, always gave first consideration to the humanities. For example, to his conclusion that underinvestment made 'this marginalization of humanities research ... a waste of national talent,' Laver quickly added: 'A similar picture applies in the arts.'[17] Similarly, sections 19 to 30 of Laver's paper developed an extensive account of 'the instrumental [economic] benefits of humanities research'. Three slight sections on 'the benefits of arts research' followed.[18] Laver's original paper recommended establishing 'a new Humanities and Arts Research Council (HARC)'.[19] The Dearing Report elaborated distinctions among research into, through, and for the arts, noting that the first 'employs methods close to those of the humanities and could reasonably be assessed by the same processes and the same criteria.'[20] Nonetheless, in the end, the report concluded in favour of establishing 'a new Arts and Humanities Research Council (AHRC)' with 'broader coverage to include research into, through, and for the arts'. Later, Laver explained that 'in the Dearing Research Group, the tide of feeling turned decisively in favour of a Research Council only when ... I was able as the

Group's humanities adviser to make a case for combining the Arts and Humanities in a joint Research Council.[21]

Given the new investment needed, the Dearing Report recommended that the budget of the new AHRC be increased to between £45 and £50 million per year over three years. This recommendation took as a baseline the £21.5 million currently disbursed through the Humanities Research Board of the British Academy.[22] But the report made the explicit point that 'the disbursement of funds in other disciplines (including some of those embraced by the British Academy) is through the Research Councils.' Later it noted 'a tension between two present roles of the British Academy — as an agent of government [disbursing humanities funding] … and as a learned body responsible for providing an independent voice across the much wider spectrum of the humanities and social sciences'.[23] Acknowledging the implication that the British Academy would have to withdraw from distributing funds, the Dearing Report's whole section on research in the arts and humanities concluded with the hope that this 'would provide the Academy with an opportunity to focus its entire attention on the needs of the humanities and social sciences, as does the Royal Society for the sciences.'[24]

Toward the end of Laver's paper, the argument had become almost lyrical in elaborating possibilities for co-operation between the proposed Research Council and the existing ones. Within his own field of language and linguistics, Laver suggested that humanist contributions to research in psycholinguistics, sociolinguistics, and applied linguistics could be co-funded with ESRC; to computational linguistics and language-based informatics with EPSRC; to speech and language pathology with MRC; to prehistoric capacity for speech with BBSRC. Warming to his topic, Laver continued that 'comparable examples for suitable joint funding of research on topics with historical dimensions are even more numerous, as are possibilities of joint funding for philosophical research on Foresight-oriented topics with ethical relevance....'[25] The main text of the Dearing Report held back from such expansive optimism, however, preferring to rest its case on fair representation for, and adequate investment in, all the disciplines.[26]

In February of 1998 the new Government published its full response to the Dearing Report. With respect to research, it 'is committed to maintaining a world class science base. It recognises the strains on the dual support system and has provided extra funding to enable universities to make a start on meeting urgent infrastructure and equipment needs for teaching and research in 1998-99.'[27] With respect to the arts and humanities in particular,

> the Government has noted the widespread support from interested organisations for the need for new arrangements for funding arts and humanities research. It is considering the Committee's recommendation for the establishment of an Arts and Humanities Research Council in the context of the Comprehensive Spending Review, taking into account the Committee's view that an additional £25m is needed ... and bearing in mind, too, the need for primary legislation to establish a new Research Council.

The Government did announce that the Higher Education Funding Council for England would set aside £8m in 1998/99 for arts and humanities research. This was to be administered by 'a new board set up by the Funding Council'. However, the new government responded to the principal recommendation made by the Dearing Report with respect to the arts and humanities — the call for an Arts and Humanities Research Council — only that 'arrangements beyond 1998/99 will be announced in due course.'[28]

NOTES

[1] Steven Kelman, *Making Public Policy: A Hopeful View of American Government* (Basic Books, 1987), pp. 38-41. Also: Michael Howlett and M. Ramesh, *Studying Public Policy: Policy Cycles and Policy Subsystems* (Toronto etc.: Oxford University Press, 1995) and James E. Anderson, *Public Policymaking* (Third Edition; Boston etc.: Houghton Mifflin Company, 1997).

[2] The Committee of Inquiry into Higher Education, *Higher Education in a Learning Society: Report of the National Committee* (July 1997), p. 1. [hereafter 'Dearing']

[3] Dearing, Annex A.

[4] Dearing, pp. 176-177.

[5] Dearing, Appendix 3, John Laver 'The need to invest in research in the humanities and the arts: Paper submitted to the Research Working Group of the National Committee', pp. 15-16. [hereafter 'Laver']

[6] Laver, p. 11.

[7] Laver, pp. 16-17.

[8] Laver, p. 17.

[9] Laver, pp. 18-19.

[10] Laver, p. 14. The £950/year figure was based on the amount of funding available annually from the HRB and the British Academy in general. The specifics of this back-of-the-envelope calculation were quite controversial; the general point—that the humanities were undercapitalized—was virtually self-evident.

[11] Laver knew whereof he wrote. Between 1984 and 1994 he had been founding Director, then Chairman of the Centre for Speech Technology Research (CSTR) at the University of Edinburgh. CSTR was a collaborative research institute, bringing together as many as fifty researchers from the three disciplines of Linguistics, Artificial Intelligence and Electrical Engineering to study speech-based human/computer interfaces. CSTR's largest project—and the largest at that time in the history of the Scottish universities—involved participation in an academic and industrial Consortium competing with similar efforts around the world to design and build automatic speech recognition and text-to-speech conversion systems. CSTR's total contract funding in the ten years exceeded £11 million. John Laver, personal communication, 21 December 2007. Clearly the British Academy, in choosing Laver to head the HRB and later to represent humanities research to the Dearing Committee, had become much more sympathetic to larger-scale projects. The seeds of this development could perhaps be traced to the enthusiastic response the Academy received when a 1987 grant from Leverhulme Trust enable it to probe unfilled demand for 'group research'. Peter Brown, personal communication, 6 December 2007.

[12] Laver, p. 14.

[13] Dearing, p. 174.

[14] Dearing, p. 175.

[15] Dearing, pp. 166-167.

[16] Dearing, pp. 165-170.

[17] Laver, p. 15.

[18] Laver, pp. 16-20.

[19] Laver, p. 23.

[20] Dearing, p. 174.

[21] Dearing, p. 175. Later, John Laver wrote: 'In the Dearing Research Group, the tide of feeling turned decisively in favour of a Research Council only when, with detailed input from Christopher Frayling, the Rector of the Royal College of Art, I was able as the Group's humanities adviser to make a case for combining the Arts and Humanities in a joint Research Council. Particularly sympathetic members of the Research Group were Howard Newby, David Watson, Adrian Webb, and Ron Dearing himself. The main committee accepted the Group's recommendation that a new Arts and Humanities Research Council should be established as soon as possible.' *Arcady* No. 5 (Spring 2002), p. 1. British Academy President Keith Thomas had nominated Laver to represent the humanities to the Dearing sub-group on research.

[22] Dearing, p. 176.

[23] Dearing, pp. 174-175.

[24] Dearing, p. 176.

[25] Laver, p. 22.

[26] Dearing, p. 175.

[27] *Higher Education for the 21st Century: Response to the Dearing Report*, Chapter 5, Introduction.

[28] *Higher Education for the 21st Century: Response to the Dearing Report*, Chapter 5, Section 6.

III

AHRB: The Early Years

The Dearing Report occasioned a great public debate and its proposal for an Arts and Humanities Research Council was not omitted from this discussion. Not all the comment was favourable. The new Commons Select Committee on Science and Technology, for example, drew an early line in the sand: 'We strongly recommend that the Government should reject any proposals that the Arts and Humanities Research Council should be placed within the structure of the Office of Science and Technology.'[1]

The 'due course' in which the Government was to respond to the Dearing Report's recommendation of an AHRC turned out to be a lengthy one. An *Annual Report* for 1998-1999 observed that 'Government has yet formally to respond to this recommendation.'[2] A year later, the report for 1999-2000 noted that 'Government has yet to make a decision on this matter.'[3] But the Government did stay with the tentative course it had announced. Speaking in September 1998, the Minister of State for Education gave a public green light to an interim board to fund arts and humanities research.[4] In the event, proponents of a new Research Council had already set off to assemble an organization that would demonstrate the worth of the full Dearing recommendation.

Clearly the Humanities Research Board of the British Academy would be part of this process, but fresh impetus came from the Higher Education Funding Council of England.[5] HEFCE had been trying to introduce a new model by which it would fund English institutions of higher education, its role in the dual support system. Unfortunately, its new formula for research, especially when combined with a major reduction in the overall allocation for 1996-97, meant less funding for humanities research. The prospect that the allocation would be reduced further in the next two years left humanists expressing 'considerable anxiety'[6] and HEFCE looking for a compromise. It could restore the lost funds by supporting specific humanities research projects, but it required some body to manage that support. The AHRC for which the Dearing Report called sounded ideal, and HEFCE entered intensive negotiations with the British Academy in June 1997. Chastened by its earlier experience with the Government, the Academy was less enthusiastic; some members were very reluctant to get involved with 'directed research'. Many months later *The Times Higher Education Supplement* could still refer to 'the collapse of the idea of an Arts and Humanities Research Council'.[7] Nonetheless Tony Wrigley, the British Academy's new President, proved a powerful advocate of a new organization, and HEFCE publicly and persuasively reversed itself to promise an additional £8 million for humanities research in 1997-98 and 1998-99.[8] Eventually, the British Academy and HEFCE signed a 'Heads of Agreement' in June 1998 that cleared the way to assembling a new organization.[9]

Paul Langford, Chair-designate of the British Academy's now superseded Humanities Research Board, was designated the first Chair and Chief Executive of the AHRB, effective 1 October when the Arts and Humanities Research Board was to commence its official existence.[10] Over the summer of 1998 he led a team of academics and administrators from both the British Academy and HEFCE to prepare the way for the new Board, to plan the creation of a research awards department in HEFCE's offices at Bristol, and to integrate the postgraduate awards section in the British Academy within the overall structure of the emerging organisation. The assistance of numerous members of the staff in both the British Academy and HEFCE was crucial to the rapid implementation of the agreement, especially that of Peter Brown in London and HEFCE's Director of Policy, Bahram Bekhradnia, in Bristol.

When the AHRB came into being in October, it had no independent legal status; it could not employ a staff or set up a bank account. Technically the new AHRB was to advise its founders—the Department for Education in Northern Ireland as well as the British Academy and the Higher Education Funding Council of England—on their funding for arts and humanities research.[11] After some suitably cautious manoeuvres, the Scottish Higher Education Funding Council and the Higher Education Funding Council of Wales announced their intentions of joining the AHRB. The effect was to ensure that from the beginning of the academic year 1999-2000, the Board could serve researchers throughout the United Kingdom, just as did the science and social science Research Councils.[12] A Funders Group with representation from all five organizations provided overall guidance for the AHRB.

From the outset the Board took as its mission to 'improve the breadth and depth of our knowledge and understanding of human culture, both past and present, and thereby enhance the quality of life and creative output of the nation.' This involved supporting research excellence in the arts and humanities, the development of highly trained people, and the dissemination of research results not only to the research community but also 'to the public at large'.[13] By the autumn of 1999, the Board was able to elaborate a strategy focused around realising the full potential of a large academic community that had limited previous experience of project funding. Its strategic aims emphasized promoting competition to ensure the highest quality, achieving balance between diverse disciplines, ensuring rigour by sophisticated peer review, developing collaboration to permit interdisciplinary research, and securing value by demonstrating the social, economic and cultural goals that the arts or humanities research would meet.[14]

Achieving these ambitions and aspirations could by no means be taken for granted. In the event of failure the Board could easily have been stood down as quickly as it had been brought into being. Much depended on the effectiveness of the AHRB, but much more depended on the way it was regarded by researchers in the vast range of arts and humanities disciplines. They were being offered new opportunities to engage in large-scale, collaborative, and practice-based projects. Despite the intentions of the British Academy, HEFCE, and the new AHRB itself, some senior academics in the humanities continued to entertain doubts about the feasibility of extensive engagement with a funding regime that might well have largesse but might also come to constrain the traditional activities of the 'lone scholar'. [15]

Effective and responsible investment of the new research funds was made very much easier by building on the experience of the British Academy's Humanities Research Board. During the summer months of 1998 the HRB panels were prepared for the new work that lay before them. They were also expanded to cope with the quantity and diversity of new applications anticipated. In the case of the creative and performing arts, new panels had to be instituted both to assess research applications and to administer the postgraduate studentships which had formerly been managed by HEFCE. The more than ninety panellists greeted responsibility for the AHRB's research and postgraduate awards with enthusiasm.[16] This successful transplantation of very high quality peer review to the new Board was a deeply important development. The AHRB itself was soon taking a quite public pride in 'the rigour, effectiveness and impartiality of its peer review process', calling it essential to uphold the organization's 'reputation for strict propriety and impartiality'.[17]

The Board was determined to ensure that the new research funding provided by HEFCE would be deployed quickly and efficiently. Administrators in the British Academy developed and presented for review a portfolio of new programmes and schemes to support the research community in the arts and humanities. They paid special attention to designing schemes suitable for and attractive to the arts community, whose practice-based researchers had little experience of applying for research support.[18] In its first year the AHRB made available research leave and research grants alongside small grants in the arts to match the British Academy's provision for humanities; in the second year it added research exchanges and fellowships in the arts to its range of schemes.[19] In the first year, 1998-99, the AHRB received 423 applications for Research Leave and funded 231 of them. Those concerned about the 'lone scholar' must have found this 55% success rate reassuring. The key test in these early years was to show sceptics both within and beyond academic life that there was genuine demand for the new opportunities. That test was met. A total of 504 applications for research grants to support specific projects was received in 1998-99. The AHRB was able to fund 199 of them for a success rate of 23%. The following year the number of applications for research grants climbed to 589, which pushed the success rate down to an alarming 19%. Overall in 1999-2000 the AHRB received 1249 applications for research awards and 3538 applications for postgraduate studentships.[20]

In the early months of 1999 the first grants approved by the AHRB generated considerable publicity for the new body. On February 25 the *Bristol Evening Post* could report that the Centre for Fine Print Research at the University of the West of England had been awarded a grant to study twentieth century reproductions.[21] A rush of local news stories followed: the *Hull Daily Mail,*[22] the *Belfast Telegraph,*[23] the *Birmingham Post,*[24] and so on. By April of 1999, the Higher Education Section in *The Guardian* was already drawing 'lessons' from the AHRB's 'first round of grants'.[25] By the spring of 2000 *Arcady* (the AHRB's newsletter) was publishing a photograph of the first winners of the AHRB's Fellowships in the Creative and Performing Arts,[26] and the *Gloucestershire Echo* was finding it appropriate to note that a local resident elevated to the peerage had served as an AHRB board member.[27] By summer a Scottish columnist was praising Aberdeen for having the 'energy, ideas, and the commitment' to fill a niche in the 'cut-throat world of academic spending' with its 'solid and comprehensive' proposal to the AHRB.[28]

The flood of high quality applications received by the Board almost as soon as it was established revealed a marked level of pent-up demand. The new HEFCE funds were hugely welcome, but it soon became clear that they were barely adequate. Michael Jubb who had been initially seconded from the British Academy to support the new organization and became the first Director of Programmes at the AHRB in 1999,[29] was quickly at work on refining, from the perspective of the dual support system, the case for increasing investment in arts and humanities research. Funding Councils provide block grants to institutions of higher education while Research Councils support specific research projects and postgraduate students. While nearly 25% of research-active university staff is in the arts and humanities, only 11% of Funding Council research support is allocated to those subjects. On the Research Council side, even with the new AHRB's £41 million annual budget, support was hardly comparable to the £850 million provided to other fields by the existing Research Councils.[30] [In fact, this is less than 5%.] This, Jubb implied, was small progress over the previous total inability of arts and humanities researchers to access Research Council funding, which had seemed unreasonable given their unfulfilled potential and the contribution they could make to the 'social, economic and cultural life of the nation'.[31]

The AHRB was committed to explaining to the public at large as to Government the full extent to which arts and humanities served society as a whole. Moreover, as a new and unfamiliar body, the Board necessarily devoted much attention to communicating with academic researchers. From the outset national symposia and regional colloquia, open to all researchers, were used to advertise and explain the AHRB's programmes. During the first two years Langford or Jubb personally visited more than one hundred institutions of higher education. In April 2000 the Board held a two-day strategic, consultative symposium for senior figures in higher education, related organisations and the media. Those present not only approved the directions adopted by the new AHRB, but made clear their commitment to the continuance and expansion of its activities. Their confidence was reflected in the Board's fully-fledged Corporate Plan published for the period 2000-2005. Following this spring symposium Chief Executive Paul Langford felt able to write in the Annual Report for 1999-2000 that it was now 'an explicit aim of the Board and its funders to develop towards full Research Council status.' [32]

During the year 2000 Langford also focused attention on developing operational capacity, so that the AHRB would be able 'to take full responsibility for its own administration' by the following year.[33] He established a Corporate Affairs Division and began building up its staff.[34] Frances Marsden arrived at the beginning of July to take responsibility for the new division.[35] The AHRB began to emanate an increasing sense of organizational responsibility. *Arcady* announced a new website, noting with gratification that visitors would be able 'to download application forms for all AHRB award schemes'.[36] The same issue of the newsletter reported on work to develop monitoring and evaluation arrangements to measure the impact of AHRB programmes in 'enhancing the quality of life and the creative output of the nation.'[37] In November *The Guardian* reported an even stronger indication of organizational *gravitas*: the AHRB was about to publish a list of departments in which PhD completion rates had fallen below 50%.[38]

On 1 October 2000 Paul Langford returned to Oxford to become Rector of Lincoln College.[39] His role at the Arts and Humanities Research Board was split in two, as had been the original design. Brian Follett, now retiring as vice-chancellor of Warwick University, became Chair of the AHRB,[40] while Professor David Eastwood from Swansea University became Chief Executive.[41] With these adjustments in place, in December 2000 the Funders Group formally announced its decision to establish the AHRB itself as an independent company and consolidate its activities in a separate office in Bristol.[42]

NOTES

[1] House of Commons Select Committee on Science and Technology, *First Report* Session 1997-98, Paragraph 98. The Select Committee was not completely opposed to the idea of an AHRC, however: 'While we do not consider that it is for us, as the Science and Technology Committee, to comment in detail on the precise arrangements for public support of research in the arts and humanities, we endorse, in principle, the establishment of an Arts and Humanities Research Council and welcome the Government's commitment to consider this in the context of the Comprehensive Spending Review.' Paragraph 97.

[2] Arts and Humanities Research Board, *Annual Report 1998-1999*, p. 4. [hereafter 'AHRB AR 98-99' etc.]

[3] AHRB AR 99-00, p. 3.

[4] AHRB AR 98-99, p. 6.

[5] As early as 1995 HEFCE showed sympathy for Laver's argument about larger-scale humanities research. It made a five-year award to the British Academy for Collaborative Research Fellowships totalling £750,000 a year (starting at £500,000 in year one). THES 2 June 1995.

[6] Michael Worton, Dean of Arts, University College London; Council of University Deans of Arts and Humanities, THES 21 March 1997.

[7] THES 6 February 1998.

[8] Wrigley, a demographer and economic historian, was then Senior Research Fellow at All Souls College, Oxford. THES 27 February 1998.

[9] Brian Fender, personal communication, 14 March 2007 and Michael Jubb personal communication, July 2007. For the 'heads of agreement' see British Academy, *Review July 1998-July 1999*, p. 48.

[10] Langford, a Welsh-born Professor of Modern History at the University of Oxford, was the author of *A Polite and Commercial People: England 1727-1783* (1989) and *Public Life and the propertied Englishman: 1689-1798* (1991). While the HRB was superseded, the British Academy itself retained responsibility for small research and conference grants in both the humanities and the social sciences as well as the support of individuals in research posts. *BA Some Documents*, p. 29. Moreover, the Academy vigorously embraced the role—in the words of the

Dearing Report—of 'a learned body responsible for providing an independent voice' and the 'opportunity to focus its entire attention on the needs of the humanities and social sciences, as does the Royal Society for the sciences'. See, for example, the Academy study cited in Chapter VII, Note 22: *That full complement of riches.*

[11] AHRB operated as an advisory unit to the funders (and all payments were made by them) until 2 April 2001. AHRB, *Report and Financial Statements for the period from 23 March 2001 to 31 March 2002* p. 4. [hereafter 'RFS 01-02' etc.]

[12] AHRB AR 98-99, p. 2.

[13] Paul Langford, personal communication, February 2008. The exact language is that subsequently employed in AHRB, *Corporate Plan 2000-2005* [no date], p. 2. [hereafter 'CP']

[14] Paul Langford, personal communication, February 2008 and CP pp. 4-19. The corporate plan for 2000-2005 gave the following summary:

Strategic Aim 1: Realising Potential To assist in enabling both individuals and groups of researchers in institutions and subject areas to realise their potential to improve the breadth and depth of our knowledge of human culture both past and present.

Strategic Aim 2: Promoting Competition To contribute to raising the quality of all activities which the Board serves by promoting informed and invigorating competition for all kinds of funding.

Strategic Aim 3: Achieving Balance To assist the broad-based development of research, postgraduate training and resources by ensuring that funds are distributed with regard to a balance of academic subjects, kinds of activity and projected outcomes.

Strategic Aim 4: Ensuring Rigour To contribute to raising standards in all the areas on which the Board's activities impinge by ensuring consistent rigour in the appraisal, assessment and monitoring of quality.

Strategic Aim 5: Developing Collaboration To add value to all activities served by the Board by developing partnership, collaboration and integration wherever possible.

Strategic Aim 6: Improving Effectiveness To enable the Board fully to carry out the requirements of the second arm of the dual-support system for research for arts and humanities as effectively as possible.

Strategic Aim 7: Securing Value To ensure the best possible use of public funds by ensuring value for money and demonstrable value in all the Board's programmes and activities.

Strategic Aim 8: Attaining Transparency To ensure the maximum effectiveness of the Board's operations and secure the fullest co-operation of all those affected by its activities by open and clear communication about its policies, procedures and processes.

[15] Paul Langford, personal communication, February 2008.

[16] THES 23 October 1998 and 22 October 1999. The eight panel areas for both Research and Postgraduate Studentships were: classics, ancient history and archaeology; visual art and media; English language and literature; medieval and modern history; modern languages; librarianship, archives, and information science; music and performing arts; and philosophy, religious studies, and law. The conveners of the eight panels sat on the Research Committee or Postgraduate Committee respectively, while the Chairs of these two committees were members of the Board itself. Originally eight panel conveners were also members of the Board.

[17] *Arcady* No. 3 (Spring 2001) pp. 2-3.

[18] Elizabeth Ollard, Assistant Secretary, Research Grants Department, British Academy (1994-2008), personal communication, February 2008.

[19] The small grants and fellowships schemes in creative and performing arts were to mirror established British Academy funding schemes in the humanities. Schemes for resource enhancement and research centres were announced later in 1999-2000, but awards were not made until the following year.

[20] AHRB AR 1998-99 Appendix 1; ARRB AR 1999-2000 Appendices 1, 3.

[21] *Bristol Evening Post*, 25 February 1999, p. 14.

[22] *Hull Daily Mail*, 24 May 1999, p. 11.

[23] *Belfast Telegraph*, 25 May 1999, p. 9.

[24] *Birmingham Post*, 7 June 1999, p. 5.

[25] *The Guardian*, 13 April 1999, 'Higher Education' xxv.

[26] *Arcady* No. 2 (Spring 2000) p. 3.

[27] *Gloucestershire Echo*, 1 April 2000, p. 3.

[28] Trevor Royle, 'Northern Lights Illuminate Celtic Past', in *The Sunday Herald*, 'Sevendays: Scotland's Political and Cultural Weekly' 30 July 2000, p. 5.

[29] *Arcady* No. 1 (Autumn 1999) p. 2.

[30] Jubb's £41 million figure does not include distinct HEFCE funding for galleries and museums.

[31] *Arcady* No. 2 (Spring 2000) p. 2.

[32] Personal communication, February 2008 and AHRB AR 99-00, p. 3.

[33] AHRB AR 99-00, p. 3.

[34] AHRB AR 00-01, p. 27.

[35] Personal communication, 22 December 2006.

[36] *Arcady* No. 2 (Spring 2000) p. 2. Before this, the forms were downloaded from the websites of the British Academy and HEFCE.

[37] *Arcady* No. 2 (Spring 2000) p. 4; AHRB AR 00-01, p. 19.

[38] *The Guardian*, 21 November 2000, 'Education' p. 15. In fact, AHRB was to limit the eligibility for further funding of departments showing no improvement in low submission rates.

[39] *The Times*, 29 November 1999, p. 20.

[40] *Coventry Evening Telegraph*, 12 July 2000, p. 10; *Arcady* No. 3 (Spring 2001) p. 1.

[41] *South Wales Evening Post*, 16 August 2000, p. 5; *Arcady* No. 3 (Spring 2001) p. 4. David Eastwood was Pro-Vice-Chancellor at the University of Wales, Swansea and Professor of Modern History. Among his publications are *Governing rural England: tradition and transformation in local government 1780–1840* (1994), *Government and community in the English provinces 1700-1870* (1997), and the co-edited *Union of Multiple Identities: The British Isles, c.1750-c.1850* (1997).

[42] AHRB AR 00-01, p. 27.

IV

AHRB on its Own

More, perhaps, than any of the other founders, the Higher Education Funding Council of England (HEFCE) was the organizational incubator for the AHRB. Brian Fender, HEFCE's Chairman, served as Chairman of the AHRB Funders Group.[1] In 1998 HEFCE had originally come up with £8 million of new funding to launch the AHRB.[2] Bahram Bekhradnia, HEFCE's Director of Policy, had played a key role in getting the new Board launched. So it was an apt description when one participant said that 'AHRB leapt out of HEFCE' in the course of 2001.[3]

At the beginning of the fiscal year—on 2 April 2001, to be precise—the AHRB became a company limited by guarantee. By September of that year, it had also gained legal status as a charity, partly so that it would be eligible for certain tax advantages. The newly independent company and charity took on new trustees, though the Funders Group and Board retained broad responsibilities.[4] The annual report for 2000-2001 had promised that the new AHRB would begin to produce its own audited Statutory Accounts[5] and a little more than one year later Deloitte & Touche had signed off on the 'Independent Auditors' Report to the Members of The Arts and Humanities Research Board Limited'.[6]

On 1 September 2001 the organization's staff formally transferred to employment by the AHRB[7] and in the ensuing year half the then total AHRB staff was recruited.[8] Early the next month, on 6 October 2001, the AHRB signed a ten-year lease on new office premises in the Whitefriars Building in Bristol.[9] Two days later the research and corporate divisions moved in, followed by the executive office on 29 October, and the postgraduate division—some of whom were moving down from the British Academy building in London—

on 3 December 2001.[10] On 1 August 2001 AHRB had begun paying its staff directly and making research awards and museum and gallery awards directly. Two months later it was also making postgraduate awards directly.[11] In short, from Spring to Autumn 2001, the AHRB had become able, as Chief Executive David Eastwood wrote, 'to employ our own staff, distribute our own funds, and operate in ways which still more closely mirror those of the research councils'. The AHRB was, as he put it, 'achieving independence'.[12]

The AHRB was also attaining full programmatic realization. Its Postgraduate Awards scheme had been pretty much taken over from the British Academy.[13] Its Programme of Museums and Galleries Awards had been transferred from HEFCE.[14] But it was in the area of Research Awards that new approaches could be established. Here, as we have seen, there were three award schemes in 1998, including the Research Leave scheme, particularly attractive to humanities scholars who sought to carry individual research work. These were followed quickly by Fellowships in the Creative and Performing Arts.[15] The 1999 Corporate Plan laid out a full portfolio involving three more funding schemes.[16] Of special import was that for Research Centres: ten awards were announced in June of 2000 with total value of £8 million; seven more awards were announced in November 2001 with a total value of over £6 million. On 13 June 2001, the AHRB had issued a press release announcing an eighth and final element in the portfolio of Research Awards: an Innovation Awards scheme. Another press release announced the actual awards on 13 December 2001.[17]

The Research Assessment Exercises conducted by HEFCE have not been particularly popular among humanities and arts researchers. But it was the 1996 RAE that helped generate evidence that humanities research was undercapitalized, that an active humanities researcher could expect to attract support of less than £950 a year. It was this situation that John Laver memorably characterized as 'a waste of national talent'. Similarly, the next

Research Assessment Exercise, in 2001, produced an equally impressive finding: the pace of grade improvement in the arts and humanities had outstripped that in any other subject domain. David Eastwood could fairly call this finding 'the notable success of the arts and humanities' and suggest that it could owe something to the opportunities and encouragement provided by the establishment of the AHRB.[18] In *The Times Higher*, one panellist for the 2001 art and design RAE attributed an 'explosion' to creation of the AHRB. 'There has been a significant increase in art research. Institutions that have an interest in this sector have adopted a much more serious approach this year. It wouldn't be surprising if there was an increase in results.'[19] Such results were announced toward the end of December 2001.

At the same time, HEFCE's parent organization, now entitled the Department for Education and Skills, invited the AHRB to submit a bid for direct funding to the 2002 Government Spending Review. It did so in January of 2002. Ambitiously, the bid requested funding to improve success rates in AHRB competitions, to invest more in the quality of research and training, and to create managed programmes in strategic areas. Perhaps most important, although the invitation had formally to do only with England, the AHRB constructed its bid on a UK-wide basis.[20] HEFCE funds only English institutions of higher education. It was the Research Councils that funded projects throughout the UK.

Eventually the AHRB would regard the next fiscal year, 2002-2003, as its 'first full year of independent operation'.[21] That of course was true, but it was possible because of the remarkable transition that had been effected during 2001. And then, with a flourish, the AHRB issued a press release on 10 January 2002 announcing that David Eastwood would become Vice-Chancellor of the University of East Anglia, a post he took up in September 2002.

NOTES

1 Fender was Chief Executive of HEFCE from 1995 to 2001. Prior to that, he was Vice-Chancellor of Keele University. He is a Fellow of both the Institute of Physics and the Royal Society of Chemistry.

2 THES 23 October 1998. As noted in Chapter III, Fender later explained that rationalizing HEFCE's research funding under a new formula reduced the amount going for the humanities. This 'new money' underlay the HEFCE investment in AHRB. Personal communication 14 March 2007. By this account, only £1.5 million should be counted as 'new' money.

3 Judith Hooper, personal communication, 26 October 2005.

4 The Board of Trustees also was the Board of Directors. Its principal committees were for audit and remuneration. AHRB AR 00-01 p. 30; AHRB AR 01-02 p. 41.

5 AHRB AR 00-01 p. 33.

6 AHRB RFS 01-02 p. 11.

7 AHRB RFS 01-02 p. 5.

8 AHRB AR 01-02 p. 39; AHRB RFS 01-02 p. 7.

9 AHRB RFS 01-02 p. 5; AHRB AR 00-01 p. 27.

10 AHRB RFS 01-02 p. 5.

11 AHRB RFS 01-02 p. 5.

12 AHRB AR 00-01 p. 5.

13 In 2001-02 £23.8 million was awarded for 1839 studentships. Six hundred and forty-six (646) were at the doctoral level, including 27 for doctorates in the creative and performing arts, an AHRB-originated programme. AHRB AR 01-02 pp. 48, 56. [Cf. AHRB RFS 01-02 p. 20, which gives the amount for studentships as £15.4 million.]

14 The AHRB made its first awards in this programme in 1999-2000. AHRB AR 99-00 p. 23. In 2001-02 $5.6 million was awarded to 15 English institutions. AHRB AR 01-02 p. 60.

15 Research Grants; Research Leave; and Small Grants in the Creative and Performing Arts. In 2001-02 these programmes received £7.4 million, £4.0 million and £317k respectively. AHRB RFS 01-02 p. 20. In 2001-02 the total for all Research Programmes was £22.0 million. AHRB AR p. 48. [Cf. AHRB RFS 01-02 p. 20, which gives the amount as £16.3 million.] In 1999-2000 AHRB first awarded Fellowships in the Creative and Performing Arts. AHRB AR 99-00 p. 3. In 2001-02 this programme received £570k. AHRB RFS 01-02 p. 20

16 Research Centres, Research Exchanges, and Resource Enhancement schemes. CP p. 5.

17 Also AHRB AR 00-01 p19; AHRB RFS 01-02 p. 6.

18 AHRB AR 01-02 p. 3.

[19] THES 7 December 2001.
[20] AHRB AR 01-02 p. 3; AHRB RFS 01-02 p. 6.
[21] AHRB AR 01-02 p. 47; AHRB RFS 01-02 p. 7.

V
New Partners

Since at least the Dearing Report, the argument in the UK in favour of strengthening humanities and arts research tended to emphasize the commonality of those fields with other disciplines. At one point David Eastwood offered the hope that development of the AHRB would help 'inter the baleful notion of "two cultures".'[1] From this point of view the 2000 appointment of Brian Follett as Chairman of the Arts and Humanities Research Board was a masterstroke.

Follett was already well known as Chairman of the 1992-1993 ESRC and British Academy inquiry on the future of funding in the humanities and social sciences,[2] but his grounding in British academic and public life went much deeper. Since 1978 he had been a professor of zoology at Bristol University with an extensive research programme on seasonal breeding in birds and mammals. From 1987 to 1993 he had served as Biological Secretary for the Royal Society—an honorary and part-time role—and from 1993 until 2001 as Vice-Chancellor of Warwick University. In 2001 Follett chaired *The Royal Society Inquiry into Infectious Diseases in Livestock*, which examined scientific aspects of the foot and mouth crisis.[3]

When AHRB Chairman Brian Follett wrote 'as a scientist it gives me singular pleasure to see my colleagues in the humanities availing themselves of these extra resources,' the public had reason to take him seriously.[4] When Follett wrote that research in the arts and humanities had demonstrated to the Government that such research is 'quite as strong as in the natural sciences and must be treated on a par with it in all respects,' the judgment was not easy to ignore. AHRB's 'non-executive' Chairman brought a commitment to its mission that reached across to new partners and allies. 'The ultimate aim must be to bring together all areas which systematically create and shape knowledge: our own "Wissenschaft".'[5]

The role of the Council for Science and Technology is to provide independent advice to the Prime Minister on strategic issues having to do with science and technology.[6] During the years 2000 and 2001, while so much was happening within the AHRB itself, a distinguished CST team led by Cambridge historian Emma Rothschild considered what bearing the arts and humanities might have on strategies for science.[7] The team consulted with John Laver, Paul Langford, Brian Fender, David Eastwood, and Brian Follett, among other leading scientists and scholars.[8] In July of 2001 the Council for Science and Technology issued their report to the Prime Minister and other government leaders. It was called *Imagination and Understanding: A Report on the Arts and Humanities in relation to Science and Technology.*

The Council found that 'the arts and humanities are an outstanding part of UK research' contributing 'in multiple ways to the nation's prosperity and wellbeing'.[9] It observed that these subjects are more intensely engaged with language than other disciplines and therefore would have a particularly important role in helping to shape 'the new communication society'.[10] But the CST's most striking argument had precisely to do with those other disciplines. 'In the circumstances of modern society and the modern global economy, the concept of a distinct frontier between science and the arts and humanities is anachronistic.'[11]

The report rejected the assumption that such a frontier was necessary or permanent; the notion rather was 'a largely European invention, of the mid Victorian period'. It made the keen historical observation that use of the word 'science' to denote only 'physical and experimental science' had been described in the 1860s as new, and particularly characteristic of 'Englishmen'. The ultimate concern of *Imagination and Understanding*, however, was not historical but strategic: 'It is in the interest of science and technology that the archaic divisions between the arts and the sciences should be questioned, and reduced.'[12]

These divisions were of concern to science, according to the CST, because many of today's most exciting areas of research lie between and across the boundaries of the traditionally defined disciplines. The archaic distinction between types of knowledge inflicted a discontinuity 'located in the middle of the disciplines of linguistics, economic history, archaeology, design and information science'.[13] Moreover, the UK's current organization of research funding—six Research Councils on the one hand and the AHRB on the other—was likely to perpetuate the distinction and 'discourage imaginative interdisciplinary research.'[14]

The CST recognized that fostering *Imagination and Understanding* would require more than reorganizing research funding. The report called also for less specialized school curricula and broader programmes of undergraduate instruction. Students in the arts and humanities, as well as researchers in those fields, would have to learn to use the new information and communication technologies. But in July 2001 the Prime Minister's Council for Science and Technology forthrightly drew the organizational conclusion from its line of thought. 'We recommend that the Arts and Humanities Research Board should now develop into a UK-wide Arts and Humanities Research Council.'[15]

From the CST's perspective of science and technology strategy, it was important that the arts and humanities be engaged more fully in discussion and implementation of national and international research priorities.[16] The AHRB should become a member of the Science and Engineering Base Coordinating Committee.[17] The current Quinquennial Review of the Research Councils should think through the consequences of creating an AHRC 'for relations between the Research Councils, DfES, and the British Academy'.[18]

On 13 February 2001 the Office of Science and Technology had announced the first Quinquennial Review of the six grant-awarding

Research Councils since their reorganization in 1994.[19] Among the independent members of the Review Steering Group was Brian Follett who was named Chair of the working group on 'relations between the Councils and their stakeholders'.[20] Made public on 19 July 2001, the first stage of the Quinquennial Review concluded that the Research Councils should continue in their existing form as executive Non-Departmental Public Bodies. It did note, however, gaps in the subject coverage provided by the existing Research Councils, especially in the area of the arts and humanities. This set a problem to be addressed in the second stage of the Review, 'how to ensure dialogue across the whole research community'.[21]

Unencumbered by having to reconsider the very existence and nature of the Research Councils, the second stage of the Quinquennial Review could look into improving their effectiveness. Released on 4 December 2001, this subsequent part of the Review highlighted the challenge of creating 'an environment in which the Research Councils operate collectively and respond flexibly to changing circumstances'.[22] The Councils needed a clearer strategic framework according to which they operate as a group, more collegiality in interacting with key partners, and improved public service delivery.[23] In short, 'the Councils should ... be capable of operating as a "virtual single Council", the boundaries and operational differences between them invisible to the people with whom they work.'[24]

The Quinquennial Review thus recommended setting up a high level 'Research Councils UK Strategy Group'[25] and explicitly requiring that each Council work in partnership not only with the other Councils but with other stakeholders. Here the AHRB came in for explicit mention.[26] Extending its integrative agenda, the Review further recommended that the outward-facing processes and practices of the Research Councils should have—unless otherwise justified—'common interfaces with the community'.[27] Internally the

Councils should share best practice and work toward 'greater harmonisation of process'.[28]

Like the Council for Science and Technology, the Quinquennial Review insisted that proper consideration of national research strategy required the voice of the arts and humanities: 'AHRB, and AHRC if created, should participate fully in RCSG.'[29] And, on the chance that the implication of its own argument was not clear enough, the Review reported that, because of the increasing importance of cross-disciplinary research, the CST 'recommends that a UK-wide Arts and Humanities Research Council (AHRC) be created. We endorse this view.'[30]

David Eastwood quickly noted the benefits that would flow to the AHRB from this 2001 Quinquennial Review of the Research Councils.[31] And, in the event, when the RCUK was set up on 1 May 2002, the AHRB was drawn in at once,[32] joining not only the RCUK Strategy Group but also its six subsidiary working groups.[33] The fledging arts and humanities research body was finding new partners.

Both *Imagination and Understanding* and the Quinquennial Review received a favourable response. *The Times Higher* noted pointedly that the Council for Science and Technology 'is chaired by trade and industry secretary Patricia Hewitt, with the government's chief scientific advisor, David King, deputising' and that its *Imagination and Understanding* 'will be taken into account in the 2002 spending review.'[34] Hewitt commented that the Quinquennial Review recommendations 'offer the prospect of even better value from our major science investments.'[35] The AHRB was invited to join not only the RCUK groups but also DTI's Science and Engineering Base Coordinating Committee (initially as an observer).[36] Settling into its new neighbourhood, the AHRB participated for the first time in the annual festival organized by the British Association for the Advancement of Science. [37]

In an Opinion piece in *The Times Higher* of 14 June 2002, Eric Evans and Jane Longmore, co-convenors of the History at Universities Defence Group, observed, 'a quiet note of optimism is, at last, apparent in the arts and humanities.' They went on, however, to excoriate continuing 'weak strategic planning', particularly at the level of individual universities.[38] For its part, the AHRB was working to co-ordinate with other organizations and to enhance its strategic focus. The AHRB's series of subject-based symposia were succeeded by research strategy seminars, focusing on issues like scholarly publishing.[39] Almost from the very beginning, the AHRB had celebrated its partnership with the Arts and Humanities Data Service;[40] now it stressed joint efforts 'to create a new and distinctive strategy' for AHDS 'development over the next three years'.[41]

The AHRB's closest neighbour among the Research Councils was the Economic and Social Research Council. Regular meetings with the ESRC had already produced joint statement on 'Interfaces between the Arts and Humanities and the Social Sciences' which included agreement to collaborate in funding research at some such interfaces.[42] By 31 January 2002 *The Times Higher* could announce the AHRB's first joint programme: 'Cultures of Consumption'. Over the next six years the ESRC and the AHRB would collaborate to invest £5 million[43] for research projects in such areas as the penetration of the domestic sphere by consumer culture; the changing boundaries between local, metropolitan, and transnational consumer cultures; and alternative and sustainable consumption.[44] The AHRB had long since expressed the hope that the agreement with the ESRC would be 'the prelude to similar arrangements with other Research Councils'.[45]

Although the Dearing Report had linked arts research with the humanities almost as an afterthought, the arts actually provided much of the early opportunity for the AHRB to forge new alliances. On-going discussions with the Design Council and the Arts Councils led to a joint programme of Arts and Science Research Fellowships for creative and performing artists who wished to collaborate with scientists. [46] The programme was co-sponsored by the AHRB and the Arts Council of England.[47] Eventually such work at the border with science and engineering led to a joint effort with another Research Council: the Engineering and Physical Sciences Research Council (EPSRC). A five-year joint initiative, 'Designing for the 21st Century', was funded for a total of £6.5 million.[48] John Laver's original argument to the Dearing Commission had stressed that, like the sciences in kind if not degree, the humanities also provided the UK with 'instrumental benefits'. The new partnership with the sciences provided the AHRB with the opportunity for further steps in that direction. It was invited to join the Foundation for Science and Technology, a group of some 500 companies, universities, government departments, and research organizations that considered policy issues having to do with science and engineering. Brian Follett, AHRB's Chairman, became a member of FST's Board.[49]

Perhaps more to the point, the AHRB joined RCUK's annual business plan competition, and, according to *The Times Higher* of 12 April 2002, even sponsored a two-day 'commercialization' workshop. While this event may have raised a few traditional humanities eyebrows, the adjoining eyes might also have noted that nearly one-third of the entries in the subsequent business plan competition came from arts and humanities fields. Perhaps the AHRB's declared intention to promote links between higher education and the creative industries eventually would realize an increase in 'instrumental benefits'.[50]

Extending its alliance building even farther, the AHRB joined the European Science Foundation in November of 2002 and began to participate in ESF's Eurocores Initiative on the 'Origins of Man, Language and Languages'.[51] The AHRB also expressed interest in helping UK researchers participate the European Union's Sixth Framework Programme of Research 'which for the first time includes specific provision for research in the humanities'.[52]

'By any stretch of the imagination it has been an excellent year and I do believe we are close to ensuring that the arts and humanities are treated in as serious a fashion as the natural and social sciences,' said Brian Follett, reflecting on the AHRB's progress in his first year.[53] Two years later, by the end of 2002 the humanities and arts in the UK were closer still to those sciences. That was neither accident nor destiny.

NOTES

[1] AHRB AR 01-02 p. 4.

[2] ESRC: Economic and Social Research Council.

[3] Follett also chaired two government enquiries concerning university libraries, one in 1993, another in 2003.

[4] AHRB AR 00-01 p. 3.

[5] AHRB AR 01-02 p. 5.

[6] Council for Science and Technology, *Imagination and Understanding*, July 2001 p. 1. [hereafter 'CST']

[7] CST p. 3. The other members were Javaid Aziz (Chief Executive, Aspective Limited), Vicki Bruce (Deputy Principal, Research and Professor of Psychology, University of Stirling), and David Potter (Chairman, Psion PLC).

[8] CST pp. 17-18.

[9] CST p. 1.

[10] CST p. 14.

[11] CST p. 1.

[12] CST p. 3.

[13] CST p. 10.

[14] CST p. 2.

[15] CST p. 2.

[16] CST p. 2.

[17] The Science and Engineering Base Coordinating Committee are in the Office of Science and Technology (OST) of the Department of Trade and Industry (DTI). CST p. 13.

[18] DfES: Department for Education and Skills (parent body of HEFCE). CST p. 13.

[19] *Quinquennial Review of the grant awarding Research Councils* Stage 1 (19 July 2001) p. 1. [hereafter '*Quinquennial Review*']; *Quinquennial Review* Stage 2 (4 Dec 2001) p. 1; *Arcady* No. 5 (Spring 2002) p. 3.

[20] *Quinquennial Review* Stage 2 pp. 90, 93, 98.

[21] *Quinquennial Review* Stage 1 p. 5.

[22] *Quinquennial Review* Stage 2 p. 1.

[23] *Quinquennial Review* Stage 2 pp. 1-2.

[24] *Quinquennial Review* Stage 2 p. 3.

[25] *Quinquennial Review* Stage 2 pp. 2, 5, 31. 'RCSG': Research Councils Strategy Group. 'RCUK': Research Councils United Kingdom.

[26] *Quinquennial Review* Stage 2 p. 29.

[27] *Quinquennial Review* Stage 2 p. 2.

[28] *Quinquennial Review* Stage 2 p. 8.

[29] *Quinquennial Review* Stage 2 pp. 5, 31.

[30] *Quinquennial Review* Stage 2 p. 30.

[31] David Eastwood in AHRB AR 01-02 p. 4.

[32] AHRC AR 2002-03 p. 12.

[33] AHRC AR 2002-03 p. 12; *Arcady* No. 5 (Spring 2002) p. 3.

[34] THES 10 August 2001 p. 4.

[35] THES 7 December 2001 p. 52.

[36] AHRB RFS 01-02 p. 6.

[37] AHRC AR 2002-03 p. 31.

[38] THES 14 June 2002 p. 16.

[39] AHRB AR 01-02 p. 36.

[40] AHRB AR 99-00 p. 11; AHRB AR 00-01 p. 10.

[41] AHRB AR 01-02 p. 8.

[42] AHRB AR 00-01 p. 10.

[43] £4 million from ESRC; £1 million from AHRB.

[44] THES 31 Jan 2002; AHRB RFS 01-02 p. 6.

[45] AHRB AR 00-01 p. 10.

[46] AHRB AR 00-01 p. 10.

[47] Because of ACE sponsorship, the fellowships were limited to artists from England. *Arcady* No. 6 (Spring 2003) p. 5.

[48] The design initiative runs from 2005 to 2009. AHRB AR 03-04 pp. 7, 11.

[49] AHRB AR 01-02 p. 37; *Arcady* No. 5 (Spring 2002) p. 2. FST took over the London space of AHRB's Postgraduate Division when it moved to Bristol.

[50] AHRB AR 01-02 p. 22; *Arcady* No. 5 (Spring 2002) p. 7; THES 12 April 02; *Arcady* No. 6 (Spring 2003) p. 4; AHRB AR 03-04 p. 11.

[51] AHRB RFS 01-02 p. 6; AHRB AR 01-02 p. 28.

[52] AHRB AR 01-02 p. 30.

[53] AHRB AR 00-01 p. 3.

VI

Under Way

By 2002-2003, its fifth year, the AHRB's total budget had risen to £64.8 million from an initial £17.9 million.[1] Throughout this period, non-programme costs were capped at five per cent.[2] Putting administrative costs aside then, in its fifth year the AHRB had programmatic expenditures of £61.7 million, more than 20% above the initially predicted £51.2 million.[3] About £9 million went to museums and galleries operated by English universities; the rest of its portfolio was distributed almost equally between postgraduate awards (£26.6m) and research awards (£26.1m) throughout the UK.[4] In the latter category long-term, focused research centres were emblematic of the new organization's direction and its dynamism.

In his 1997 report to the Dearing Committee, John Laver had criticized vigorously the 'straight-jacket of humanities research funding' that restricted a research-active member of a UK humanities faculty—almost inevitably a sole-practitioner.[5] The AHRB's new research centres aimed to address such underinvestment. In 2000 the Board announced multi-year awards to fund ten research centres at an average of £800,000 each. In 2001 it announced the funding of an additional seven centres, and in 2002 two more. All told, the AHRB committed £16 million to supporting nineteen humanities and arts research centres for five years each. From Aberdeen to Belfast to Canterbury, from British Film and Television to the Evolutionary Analysis of Cultural Behaviour, and from Asian and African Literatures to Intellectual Property, resources were being concentrated to heighten the effectiveness of arts and humanities research.

Intellectual ambitions rose with the funding. The AHRB Centre for Editing Lives and Letters began with editing Francis Bacon but sought to disseminate protocols and best practice for scholarly editing in the digital age.[6] The Centre for British Film and Television Studies aimed, among other goals, 'to make an authoritative contribution to public policy relating to film and television in Britain and Europe'.[7] The AHRB Centre for Irish and Scottish Studies involved a partnership among the University of Aberdeen, Queen's University, Belfast, and Trinity College, Dublin. The AHRB annual report described its work in these words:

> Devolution has created an impetus towards greater understanding of the various factors which have shaped modern attitudes and politics. Irish-Scottish Studies seeks to demythologise our history and culture in areas of contemporary concern—concerns which have fashioned a host of connections within the islands of Britain.[8]

Similar themes were sounded in other research programmes. His AHRB Research Grant meant, reported one archaeologist working on a long-delayed multinational project in Romania, that the team was 'able to plan a systematic long-term investigation with the confidence that we actually have the core funding needed to accomplish our goals'.[9] A law professor at Queen's University, Belfast, had helped foster community-based dispute resolution as a means of supplanting paramilitary punishment. An AHRB-supported Research Leave in the Human Rights Program at Harvard Law School enabled him to develop a more widely accessible discussion of restorative justice and its relation to ideas of human rights and transitional justice.[10]

AHRB awards started to fill out the vast domain from the arts to neighbouring sciences. Puzzlement about what might constitute research in the creative and performing arts began to be dispelled by such projects as one having to do with printmaking and 'using modified primary colours to create the surface contour of an object'.[11]

Another AHRB-funded project used DNA analysis to identify the animal skin from which various pieces of medieval parchment were made.[12] Researchers in Scotland's languages received a £160k grant from Engineering and Physical Sciences Research Council; they built on it to win a subsequent £300k award from the AHRB.[13]

The AHRB appeared to be working to bring to the arts and humanities the benefits of more intense concentration classically analysed in Derrick J. De Solla Price's 1963 *Little Science, Big Science.* It estimated, for example, that 600 contract researchers were employed on AHRB-supported projects at the end of March 2002.[14] That year it announced a series of workshops for directors of AHRB Research Centres 'to enable them to learn from each others' experiences in managing collaborative research on a scale that, until now, has been rare in the arts and humanities'.[15]

The same interest in concentration had begun to appear in the other major part of the AHRB portfolio: postgraduate awards. Here £26.6 million supported 2500 arts and humanities graduate students in 2002-03.[16] In science fields graduate training typically involves work on a portion of a mentor's research project. While stressing that it was not abandoning wholesale the humanities' more individualistic approach to graduate training, the AHRB did open the door a bit to the more collaborative approach of the sciences. In 1999 it began to allow projects it supported to replace research assistants with project-based doctoral students.[17] In 2000 it allowed directors of large-scale projects to apply for doctoral studentships to be attached to those projects.[18] Even in a University of St. Andrews neo-Fregean investigation of the nature of mathematical knowledge, the AHRB supported two postgraduate studentships 'working on specific well-defined "subprojects" within the overall scheme'.[19]

And so, by its fifth year, the AHRB emanated a distinct sense of direction and momentum. Applications for research funding had risen 58% over three years. Applications for postgraduate awards had gone up 20% in a single year.[20] The four-year doctoral submission rate for students in the arts and humanities stood at 78%.[21] Ten years earlier it had been 34%.[22] Again, earlier words from an AHRB official—this time from Chief Executive David Eastwood— can be borrowed to characterize the emerging organization: 'Quite rightly, the AHRB has been expected to prove itself and to establish the case for a fully-fledged research council. This we believe we have achieved.'[23]

NOTES

[1] The £17.9 million amount was for less than a full year. An early pattern was established in which 77% of programmatic funding went into humanities awards, 23% into arts. AHRB AR 98-99 p. 9.

[2] David Eastwood, AHRB AR 00-01 p. 5.

[3] AHRB AR 98-99 p. 17.

[4] AHRB AR 02-03 p. 38.

[5] Cf. Chapter II, pp. 10.

[6] AHRC AR 2002-03 p. 16.

[7] AHRB AR 00-01 p. 16.

[8] AHRB AR 00-01 p. 20.

[9] *Arcady* No. 6 (Spring 2003) p. 3.

[10] AHRB AR 01-02 p. 35.

[11] AHRB AR 00-01 p. 21.

[12] AHRC AR 2002-03 p. 14.

[13] THES 17 Dec 2004.

[14] AHRB AR 01-02 p. 16.

[15] AHRB AR 01-02 p. 6. *Arcady* No. 7 (Summer 2003) p. 8.

[16] AHRC AR 2002-03 p. 18.

[17] AHRB AR 99-00 p. 14.

[18] AHRB AR 00-01 p. 14.

[19] AHRB AR 99-00 p. 13.

[20] David Eastwood AHRB AR 01-02 p. 3. The three years were 99-00, 00-01, 01-02; the single year was from 00-01 to 01-02.

[21] AHRC AR 2002-03 p. 19. *Arcady* No. 7 (Summer 2003) p. 8.

[22] AHRB AR 00-01 p. 6.

[23] David Eastwood, AHRB AR 00-01 p. 5.

VII

Resistance

When the Dearing Report first appeared, the University of Oxford rumbled that 'We stand by our previously expressed opposition ... to the establishment of an Arts and Humanities Research Council (AHRC). We remain extremely doubtful whether it would result in new public funding being made available ... and we do not believe that there would be advantages in transferring control of expenditure away from the universities to a council envisaged as the instrument of a "national policy" for research in the arts and humanities.'[1] The University of Cambridge took a slightly less adamant tone. 'Reservations have previously been expressed from Cambridge about the possible establishment of a Humanities Research Council, particularly because of doubts about a directive programme basis for humanities research. ... If, however, the Arts and Humanities Research Council proposed by Dearing is not financed in any part by transfer from HEFCE the Council would not oppose it.' But the *modus operandi* of the proposed council, Cambridge said, would have to be different from the existing Research Councils. Individual research had an important and appropriate role in the humanities. And if the new council were to include art and design, that would require even more novel ways of operating.[2]

Movement toward a new Research Council not only encountered resistance from more traditional views of humanities scholarship, but also ran against a powerful current in contemporary UK political life: devolution. While reserving certain powers to the UK Parliament, the Scotland Act 1998, the Government of Wales Act 1998, and the Northern Ireland Act 1998 — in somewhat asymmetrical ways — transferred the exercise of other powers out of Westminster. Education was quite clearly among the devolved powers, and we have already seen how it took a while longer for the Scottish Higher Education Funding Council and the Higher Education Funding Council of Wales to join in support of the AHRB. But devolution is perhaps even more a matter of national spirit than it is of law. Many humanities subjects, Scottish Studies for instance, are intimately involved with that spirit. Changes in associated administrative arrangements can evoke unusual turbulence. Discussion of shifting administration of Scottish postgraduate study awards to the AHRB brought the following headline in Glasgow: 'Scots "will lose out" on graduate grants; Professor alleges sell-out over switch to English panel.'[3]

In other quarters the prospect of an AHRC received a mixed reaction. The then chief executive of the Economic and Social Research Council observed that the Dearing recommendation would be a 'historic' opportunity, but warned: 'We need to look closely at the financial details. We would not want the AHRC to be funded at the expense of the social sciences or the science base as a whole.' [4] Later the Chairman of the Standing Conference of the Heads of Schools of Architecture wrote to the AHRB to complain that the new body had perpetuated the miscategorization of architecture by the earlier Research Assessment Exercise.[5] Some politicians and cultural pundits could not resist grave—and very public—concern that a £12,252 Research Leave grant (less than 0.02% of the AHRB's budget that year) would help a scholar looking into the marginalization of lesbians as compared to gay men in French literature.[6]

Some criticism of the AHRB seemed more journalistic fun than serious opposition. When the *Scottish Daily Record* reported that environmental historians received nearly £900,000 for a four-year study of 'the history of UK rubbish', its headline was a writer's reflex: 'It's a dirty job, but…' [7] For a headline writer at the Liverpool *Daily Post* this award was obviously 'Trash Cash'.[8] Even after these sallies from fellow journalists, *The Guardian* did not hesitate to ask, 'Do academics spend their days thinking up weird titles for research?'[9]

Other criticism found a mark in the case being made for an Arts and Humanities Research Council. The Royal Society of Chemistry argued to a committee of the House of Commons that growing interdisciplinarity in science meant that the four 'scientific' Research Councils should be merged, leaving the arts and humanities, like medical research and economic and social research, on the outside.[10] A teaching assistant warned in *The Times Higher* that, by insisting on speedier completion of the PhD, the AHRB would leave new scholars unprepared at least 'in the specific field of contemporary literary theory, often informed by the complex and difficult relationship between French and German philosophy'.[11]

Since the case for creating an AHRC amounted to a series of *sed contra* exceptions to traditional assumptions, the AHRB itself was necessarily tentative in translating that case into organizational practice. To hold that humanities research was undercapitalized *was* to take exception to the normal assumption that the humanities scholar was a sole practitioner whose key resource was time. At the same time, all those individual arts and humanities researchers were an essential component of the AHRB's constituency and the emerging organization seemed a bit jumpy about making them feel included. Its first annual report emphasized that the Board 'will aim to preserve a proper balance between different modes of research, ranging from large collaborations to research conducted by individuals. ... Particular care will be taken to foster the values of originality, imaginativeness and individualism that inform research in many of its subject areas.'[12] The second annual report was nearly apologetic that the Board 'naturally' supported much project and team-work and went on to assure readers that 'the Board does not wish in any way, however, to imply a lesser commitment to other kinds of scholarship and creativity that have stood the test of time. Support for the individual researcher is provided.'[13]

Similarly, to hold that the arts and humanities brought instrumental benefits as well as intrinsic ones *was* to direct attention beyond the research work itself to some additional result. But what that result was, and how it might constitute a benefit, was yet to be illuminated. The second annual report included a section on 'Outcomes in 1999–2000' but in fact it listed only awards made and new award schemes developed.[14] Four years later the annual report's section on 'What our Awards Deliver' detailed the results of two opinion surveys. One asked research grantees about increased collaboration in arts and humanities research, the other asked how satisfied recent PhDs were with their AHRB-supported study. This report on 2003-2004 did also provide a tabulation of properly named 'outputs' (books, articles, datasets, performances, etc.),[15] but the connection between research grants in the arts and humanities, on the one hand, and economic and social benefits, on the other, was hardly a compelling straight line.

The usual assumption that 'knowledge transfer' was the link between research and economic benefit made the intellectual capital argument particularly troublesome in the case of the arts. On the one hand, it was relatively easy to point out that 'growth in the creative industries … [is] three times faster than in the economy as a whole.'[16] On the other hand, it seemed less plausible to attribute the economic success of, say, dance in the UK to the transfer of knowledge generated by research than to 'rich training environments', as one critic put it. He commented in *The Times Higher* 'the idea that the intellectual standard of dance academics has somehow transformed the quality of the UK's dance culture is laughable.'[17] Furthermore, an effort by the AHRC to foster written documentation and assessment of new knowledge generated in performance-based research could easily be taken as disregard for the actual performance, and thereby make performers 'furious'.[18]

In truth, while the macro-economic contribution of the arts and humanities to social benefit is plausible and fairly easy to illustrate, the micro-economic processes by which knowledge, especially in the arts and humanities, leads to increased wealth or even improved welfare is not yet well articulated. Thus the AHRB was left to improvise accounts of how its investments in knowledge would work out beneficially. The description of individual awards in the AHRB's initial annual report began bravely by outlining a research project that 'considers how an individual's conceptual system might be structured by metaphor.' Another project builds research infrastructure by supporting the day-to-day running and further development of a database and website. Another is said to involve a trip to Sicily, but only because it requires sources 'usually kept within Italian academic institutions'. But the report's energy for explanation inevitably ebbs. Another project's research 'will be disseminated in English and Spanish' as well as on a CD-ROM; another award will enable a scholar 'to finish work on her book'; and yet another awardee has found 'that his activity as an artist has continually informed his work as a teacher and lecturer'.[19] Two years later the annual report has a strong section on communications and public understanding, but it focuses on disseminating knowledge about support of — rather than from — arts and humanities research.[20] Two years after that, the annual report is still wrestling on the fly with the same issue, suggesting that the dissemination of arts and humanities research is better characterized as 'knowledge interaction' than as 'knowledge transfer'.[21] In sum, the state of knowledge itself resisted the AHRB's efforts to make a consistent and conclusive case that generating knowledge in the arts and humanities is a public good.[22]

NOTES

[1] *Oxford University Gazette*, 'Report of the National Committee of Inquiry into Higher Education (Dearing Report) Supplement (1) to Gazette No. 4449', Wednesday, 15 October 1997.
[2] *Cambridge Reporter*, 'National Committee of Inquiry into Higher Education: Notice', 1 October 1997.

[3] *The Herald* (Glasgow) 5 December 2001 p. 10. In fact, the awards were transferred the following year. AHRB AR 2002-03 p. 19.

[4] THES 25 July 1997 p. 5.

[5] THES 21 August 1998 p. 4.

[6] *Daily Mail* (London) 20 July 2000 p. 7; *Scottish Daily Record* 20 July 2000 p. 23; *The Herald* (Glasgow) 20 July 2000 p. 12.

[7] *Scottish Daily Record* 23 November 2001 p. 29.

[8] *Daily Post* (Liverpool) 23 November 2001 p. 19.

[9] *The Guardian* (London) 11 December 2001 'Education' p. 11.

[10] THES 18 July 2003 p. 5.

[11] THES 19 April 2002.

[12] AHRB AR 98-99 p. 8.

[13] AHRB AR 99-00 p. 9.

[14] AHRB AR 99-00 p. 25.

[15] AHRB AR 03-04 p. 50.

[16] THES 26 July 2002.

[17] THES 2 May 2003.

[18] THES 28 November 2003.

[19] AHRB AR 98-99 pp. 14-15.

[20] AHRB AR 01-02 p. 36.

[21] AHRC AR 2002-03 p. 6.

[22] For the best effort yet to address this matter see: The British Academy, *'That full complement of riches': the contributions of the arts, humanities and social sciences to the nation's wealth* January 2004. For a contrasting long-term strategy see The American Academy of Arts and Sciences, Humanities Indicators Project. For a fuller sense of the current technical gap in understanding the relation between the generation of knowledge and the creation of economic and social benefits, see the National Science Foundation Program Solicitation 07-547 which seeks projects to 'foster the development of the knowledge, theories, data, tools, and human capital needed to cultivate a new Science of Science and Innovation Policy (SciSIP). SciSIP will underwrite fundamental research that creates new explanatory models and analytic tools designed to inform the nation's public and private sectors about the processes through which investments in science and engineering (S&E) research are transformed into social and economic outcomes... Characterizing the dynamics of discovery and innovation is important for developing valid metrics, for predicting future returns on investments, for constructing fruitful policies, and for developing new forms of workforce education and training.'

VIII

In Due Course: The Government Decides

The swirl of achievement, aspiration, and resistance in the early experience of the AHRB gelled quickly. Margaret Hodge, Minister for Lifelong Learning and Higher Education in the UK Department of Education and Skills, announced a Review of Arts and Humanities Research Funding to be carried out on behalf of the Ministers responsible for higher education in England, Northern Ireland, Scotland and Wales.[1] The review would recommend how to enhance support for the arts and humanities as well as how to strengthen the advice government received on relevant issues. It would also be concerned with ensuring high quality service in these areas.[2] The review began with a formal consultation. When the 117 responses to the *Invitation to Contribute to the Review* were received by the deadline of 1 February 2002, it amounted to a referendum on AHRB efforts.

Eighty-two of these responses were from institutions of higher education (70%) and 27 from other organizations (23%). There were also five responses from academic departments and three from individual academic staff. Eleven responses were from institutions of higher education in Scotland, six from such institutions in Wales, and two more from Northern Ireland.[3] All respondents were asked if an organization was needed to make grants for arts and humanities research and how best to constitute such a body. They were also asked how the body should relate to the four territories of the UK and to the Government.[4]

Of the 117 respondents, 114 (97%) indicated the need for such an organization. There was no negative response.[5] Seventy-seven (66%) thought the AHRB had already shown itself to be effective in addressing this need[6] and 109 (93%) favoured reconstituting the AHRB as a Research Council. Strikingly, these 109 affirmative voices included all 19 of the higher education institutions responding from Scotland, Wales, and Northern Ireland.[7]

Perhaps the most impressive statement about whether the new Research Council should operate on a UK-wide basis came from the Royal Society of Edinburgh.

> While there needs to be continued support for distinctive, regional needs in terms of culture, employment structure and institutions, the Society is against the separation of Scottish research from its UK and wider nexus. … There might be a real danger of marginalisation, particularly for the vigorous, but relatively small Scottish and Welsh academic sectors, if political considerations were to inhibit this process of transfer.[8]

This laudable commitment to unimpeded research, to the simultaneous universality and particularity of the humanities and arts, was echoed by the University of Wales at Bangor.

> Academic staff … do not wish to receive *special* consideration — and certainly no ring-fenced funding — but do wish to be assured of appropriate and equitable consideration of culturally-specific projects.[9]

Overall, none of the 117 respondents said that the new Research Council should operate on other than a UK-wide basis and 94 (80%) explicitly supported UK-wide operation. Those 94 respondents included 18 of the 19 Scottish, Welsh, and Northern Irish institutions of higher education.[10] The other Research Councils operated on a UK-wide basis from their location in the Office of Science and Technology in the UK Department of Trade and Industry. Of the 91 respondents who explicitly addressed the question of where the new council should be located in the governmental structure, 60 (66%)

preferred the Office of Science and Technology and 9 other respondents (10%) mentioned OST among the acceptable possibilities.[11]

This consultation and additional evidence were taken into account by the Review itself, which was charged to consider how the experience of the AHRB could be built upon: whether the AHRB's constitution, status, or mechanisms for supporting arts and humanities research required modification.[12] The 15-member Review Steering Group was chaired by Nick Sanders of the Department for Education and Skills, and included representatives from the Department of Culture, Media and Sport and DTI's Office of Science and Technology as well as from the four higher education funding bodies. David Eastwood, Chief Executive of the AHRB, Peter Brown, Secretary of the British Academy, Colin Lucas, Vice-Chancellor of Oxford, and Roderick Floud, Provost of London Guildhall University, were also members. Cliff Nelson of the Department of Education and Skills was Secretary to the Steering Group and a key participant in pulling together its report.[13] The finished report to the Education Ministers was published in July 2002.

The Report of the Steering Group conveyed their 'overriding impression that its constituency has been considerably impressed with the AHRB'.[14] It noted that 'considerable momentum' had been built up 'stemming largely from an increased consciousness that the arts and humanities should play their proper part in the evolution of research policy and the execution of research goals.'[15] The group had concluded, 'Tests of the national interest can and should be applied to research in the arts and humanities, as with other fields.'[16]

The Steering Group focused attention on what the Dearing Report had called 'prospective funding' (as opposed to the retrospective approach of HEFCE and the other higher education funding bodies). The AHRB 'has done much in its short life since 1998 to establish the merits of a system for competitive awards of research grants and post-graduate awards in the arts and humanities.'[17] Among the reasons for adopting a UK-wide approach, 'Issues of equity, being part of wider disciplinary communities, enabling funding for collaboration across territorial as well as disciplinary boundaries, and – significantly for many – being exposed to competition in order to assure quality standards were all important.'[18] One advantage of locating the new Research Council among the others linked to OST was the 'well established systems (which have already been imported and adapted by the AHRB) for competitive procedures for research awards'.[19]

While the AHRB had made a very strong start despite its provisional and anomalous status 'in the longer term it will increasingly appear to be a deliberate ploy to treat arts and humanities research as different from, and inferior to, the more scientific disciplines.'[20] The Steering Group had explored the proposed OST location with the heads of the Research Councils and with the UK Science and Engineering Base Coordinating Committee. Both 'saw challenges as well as important opportunities. ... But the general view was that any such proposal should be supported.'[21] Taking everything into account,

> **we consider that inclusion of the Arts & Humanities Research Council, with the other Research Councils, under the aegis of the Office for Science and Technology will offer the best prospect of furthering research in the arts and humanities and permitting such research to play its fullest part in enhancing national life.** [*emphasis in original*] [22]

In arriving at this conclusion the Steering Group had worked out several adjustments that could smooth the way of the proposed AHRC. The existing responsibility of OST to promote public understanding of science would not be broadened to include the arts and humanities.[23] The AHRC charter 'should explicitly include a duty to promote research into cultural aspects of the various parts of the UK.' The new Council should meet not only in England but also in Northern Ireland, Scotland and Wales.[24] The current predominance of academic over non-academic members in the AHRB should be preserved in the new Council for five years.[25] 'Though we believe there may be advantage in due course in including a rather higher proportion of "users" of research, as is the case with some other Research Councils … more needs to be done to identify and exploit the true user base for arts and humanities research.'[26]

The Steering Group seemed conscious that it was displacing significant responsibility to the organization itself. Even if it meant temporarily exceeding the 5% limit on administrative costs, 'the current AHRB's senior management should be strengthened to permit increased capacity to liaise externally, particularly in order to develop links with the users of arts and humanities research, with the academic communities in the various parts of the UK, and with the other Research Councils.'[27]

The Report … to the Education Ministers did not directly address the long-vexed issue of individual scholarship in the humanities. But it reported that in the consultation the AHRB's schemes for individual research leave and for postgraduate awards in the arts 'were most commonly singled out as making an important difference.'[28] And it did quote the admonition from Cambridge that not all humanities research could be supported by funding projects.[29]

Nonetheless, writing in the AHRB annual report, David Eastwood exulted that 'perhaps the most significant development over the past 12 months was the Review of Arts and Humanities Funding.' Ministers would soon respond to the report, he noted.[30] Perhaps he was already celebrating the response from the Vice-Chancellor of the University of Oxford.

> I warmly endorse the report's recommendations... The AHRB has played a pivotal role in enhancing the quality of

research in arts and humanities throughout the UK. Its translation to research council status will enable it both to raise its profile and to make a still more significant contribution to research and research policy in the UK.[31]

The Ministers' response came on 22 January 2003. By then David Eastwood had departed the AHRB to become Vice-Chancellor of the University of East Anglia. He was succeeded as Chief Executive by Geoffrey Crossick, the third successive historian to hold the post. Crossick had held a Chair in History at the University of Essex since 1991 and had been Pro-Vice-Chancellor there since 1997.[32]

*

On Wednesday afternoon, 22 January 2003, barely two months before the end of the AHRB's fifth year, Education and Skills Secretary Charles Clarke took the floor of the House of Commons to announce new Government policy for higher education in England. That policy, he said, was animated by two ambitions: to better harness knowledge to wealth creation and to extend more widely the opportunity for higher education.[33] He reiterated that Government sought to increase participation in higher education toward half the 18-30 years-old age group by the end of the decade.[34] Standing in the way was a social class gap that Clarke termed 'a national disgrace'.[35] The dimensions of that gap were laid out in a White Paper released simultaneously: 'Those from the top three social classes are almost three times as likely to enter higher education as those from the bottom three. ... At the extremes, the picture is worse. Young people from professional backgrounds are over five times more likely to enter higher education than those from unskilled backgrounds.'[36]

Moreover, the new Government higher education policy aspired to 'crack' what Clarke called 'the real British disease—which is that our world-class intellectual research is exploited by competitors from other countries but not ourselves'.[37] Fulfilling this ambition would require attending to the process of knowledge transfer from research to business. The accompanying White Paper lamented that, while the proportion of businesses making innovations with the help of information from higher education had increased recently to 16%, 'this is still a small minority.'[38]

Thus, on first hearing, Clarke's announcement might have seemed a far cry from a call to establish an Arts and Humanities Research Council. The new higher education policy primarily concerned England, not the entire United Kingdom.[39] Further, among what Clarke identified as the three missions of higher education — research, knowledge transfer, teaching[40] — the policy's goal was to rebalance the years of emphasis on research that 'has, for understandable reasons, been at the expense of teaching and knowledge transfer.'[41] Even when the White Paper touched on research and 'the danger of decline', there was no mention of the arts and humanities.[42] Finally, like the Dearing Report, the central — and highly controversial — focus of the new policy was how to pay for further improvement in higher education. The minister quickly and forthrightly acknowledged 'the students' share of the overall costs of University education will increase.'[43] And yet, before he left the topic of research to discuss the Government's ambitions for knowledge transfer and teaching, Clarke promised the Commons a modestly expensive improvement: 'we will create a UK-wide Arts and Humanities Research Council to ensure that funding for the Arts and Humanities is given the status it deserves.'[44]

The Future of Higher Education, the simultaneous and more detailed White Paper, argued for these proposals from the perspective of the Government's general 'intellectual capital' or 'knowledge society' strategy. The UK could build on a comparative advantage: though it had just 1 per cent of the world's population, it produced 8 per cent of the scientific publications and 13 per cent of the most highly cited ones.[45] Every £1 million of economic output from higher education generated a further £1.5 million in other sectors of the economy.[46] Workers with a higher education earned higher salaries. Crucially, 'despite the rise in the numbers participating in higher education, the average salary premium has not declined over time and remains the highest in the OECD. It is not the case that "more means worse".'[47] Indeed, the Government's point was that more higher education could mean more real wealth.

Because a growing economy focused more of its gains in the hands of the educated, it was fair to ask more people to invest in more of their own education. In addition to Clarke's two ambitions — of expanding educational opportunity and increasing knowledge transfer — the White Paper underlines a third challenge:

> to make the system for supporting students fairer. Having a university education brings big benefits and while the Government will continue to pay most of the cost involved in studying for a degree, it is also reasonable to ask students to contribute to this.[48]

The Future of Higher Education devoted a bare two paragraphs amongst its 106 pages to the question of creating an Arts and Humanities Research Council. It invoked the conclusions of the earlier *Review of Arts and Humanities Research Funding* and asserted that 'Research in the arts and humanities is of vital importance to our university system and its international standing.' It was not just with respect to scientific and technical knowledge that research underlies innovation and innovation improves growth, productivity and quality of life. 'Research in the social sciences and in the arts and humanities can also benefit the economy — for example, in tourism, social and economic trends, design, law, and the performing arts — not to speak of enriching our culture more widely.'[49] From this perspective it could seem plausible to propose that funding for research in the arts and humanities be organized alongside that for science and technology.[50] This approach would lead to 'stronger links between researchers in different disciplines, more participation by the arts and humanities in national and international programmes and reduced bureaucracy for institutions as AHRC systems are aligned with those of the other research councils.'[51]

It must be noted that in trying to 'think carefully' about managing research funding 'in the most effective way', *The Future of Higher Education* went beyond previous appreciation of 'big science'.[52] The White Paper insisted, 'Concentration brings real benefits,' pointing to better infrastructure and collaborative publication,[53] and adding, 'some of these points are equally valid for the arts and humanities as for science and technology.'[54] This argument about concentration morphed perhaps too easily into an expectation of institutional differentiation. 'About 75 per cent of HEFCE research funding goes to the top 25 institutions, and research council grant funding follows a similar pattern. This means that some institutions have a high concentration of top quality research.'[55] Here the competitive peer review employed by the Research Councils is taken simply as an indicator rather than as a mechanism for achieving excellent research. In any case, the new emphasis for all universities is to be on teaching; the other missions of higher education are to be distributed among them.

> Our vision is of a sector which … acknowledges and celebrates the differences between institutions as each defines and implements its own mission. We see all HEIs excelling in teaching and reaching out to low participation groups, coupled with strengths in one or more of: research; knowledge transfer; linking to the local and regional economy; and providing clear opportunities for students to progress.[56]

Nonetheless, on 22 January 2003, the Government had committed to establishing an Arts and Humanities Research Council as soon as the legislative timetable permitted. Its rationale may have been muddled, but its clear aim was 'a fully functioning, statutory research council by 2005'.[57] The new AHRB Chief Executive, Geoffrey Crossick, recalled stepping out of a meeting to take a telephone call.

> Charles Clarke had just told the House of Commons of the Government's intention to establish an Arts and Humanities Research Council. I went back into the room, and repeated the message that I had just received. Everyone burst into applause, and the applause went on. I must admit that I was taken by surprise but very agreeably so … the academics on our Research Committee had remembered that this was a truly momentous moment for arts and humanities research in the United Kingdom. A moment worthy of our applause.[58]

NOTES

[1] AHRB RFS 01-02 p. 5.
[2] Department for Education and Skills, *Invitation to Contribute to the Review* (2001) p. 2. [hereafter 'Invitation']
[3] Department for Education and Skills *et al.*, *Review of Arts and Humanities Research Funding: Report of the Steering Group to Education Ministers* (2002) p.53. [hereafter 'Review']
[4] Invitation p. 5.
[5] Review p. 53.
[6] Review p. 54.
[7] Review p. 55.
[8] Review p. 34.
[9] Review p. 33.
[10] Review p. 33.
[11] Review p. 40.
[12] Invitation p. 2.

[13] Review pp. 52, 6.

[14] Review p. 28.

[15] Review p. 3.

[16] Review p. 25.

[17] Review p. 3.

[18] Review p. 33.

[19] Review p. 39.

[20] Review p. 29.

[21] Review p. 42

[22] Review p. 42.

[23] Review pp. 4, 45.

[24] Review pp. 4, 44.

[25] Review pp. 4, 44. AHRB's first Board of Management meeting for 2003 was scheduled for Edinburgh. AHRB AR 01-02 p. 37.

[26] Review p. 44.

[27] Review pp. 5, 48.

[28] Review p. 54.

[29] Review p. 54.

[30] David Eastwood, AHRB AR 01-02 p. 3.

[31] AHRB press release 22 July 2002.

[32] *Arcady* No. 6 (Spring 2003) p. 11. Crossick specializes in the social history of Britain and continental Europe in the 19th and early 20th centuries. Among many other publications, Crossick is the author of *Artisan Elite in Victorian Society: Kentish London 1840-1880* (1978) and co-editor of *Cathedrals of Consumption: the European Department Store, 1850-1939* (1999).

[33] Charles Clarke, Statement to Commons, 22 January 2003 p. 1.

[34] Charles Clarke, Statement to Commons, 22 January 2003 p. 3.

[35] Charles Clarke, Statement to Commons, 22 January 2003 p. 4.

[36] Department for Education and Skills, *The Future of Higher Education* January 2003 p. 17. [hereafter 'White Paper']

[37] Charles Clarke, Statement to Commons, 22 January 2003 p. 2.

[38] White Paper p. 15.

[39] White Paper i.

[40] Charles Clarke, Statement to Commons, 22 January 2003 p. 2.

[41] Charles Clarke, Statement to Commons, 22 January 2003 p. 2.

[42] White Paper pp. 13-14.

[43] Charles Clarke, Statement to Commons, 22 January 2003 p. 1.

[44] Charles Clarke, Statement to Commons, 22 January 2003 p. 2.

[45] White Paper p. 10.

[46] White Paper p. 10.

[47] White Paper p. 12.
[48] White Paper p. 2.
[49] White Paper p. 23.
[50] White Paper p. 24.
[51] White Paper p. 32. Here is the full text of the recommendation:

The Creation of an Arts and Humanities Research Council

2.22 Research in the arts and humanities is of vital importance to our university system and its international standing. At present, research in the arts and humanities is funded by the Arts and Humanities Research Board (AHRB) (as well as through HEFCE), rather than by a research council. In September 2001, the Government and devolved administrations launched a review of arts and humanities funding. The aim of the review was to enhance provision of arts and humanities research, and to ensure that there are no artificial barriers to interdisciplinary work between the arts and sciences, as well as to make sure that the arts and humanities are properly resourced and supported.

2.23 This review concluded that the AHRB should take on the status of a fully fledged research council funded by the Office of Science and Technology in the same way as the other research councils. This recommendation will be put into action as the legislative timetable allows, with the aim of achieving a fully functioning, statutory research council by 2005. We expect the benefits to include stronger links between researchers in different disciplines, more participation by the arts and humanities in national and international programmes and reduced bureaucracy for institutions as AHRC systems are aligned with those of the other research councils.

[52] White Paper p. 23.
[53] White Paper p. 28.
[54] White Paper p. 29.
[55] White Paper p. 26.
[56] White Paper pp. 21-22.
[57] White Paper p. 32.
[58] *Arcady* No. 6 (Spring 2003) p. 12.

IX

At the Point of a Larger Conflict

The 22 January 2003 White Paper on the Future of Higher Education produced a major uproar and a small surprise. Much of the uproar concerned 'top-up fees' — the Government's proposal to allow universities to raise fees and to provide deferred loans by which students might meet those charges. This step toward a market model of financing higher education involved the possibility of differential charges for various courses of study and for various institutions. The consequent spectre of a 'two-tier' system of higher education was reinforced by the Government's declared intention to concentrate research funding which itself added to the uproar.

Amidst the din, the White Paper's call to establish a Research Council for the arts and humanities was barely heard, at least at first. *The Guardian* headlined 'Higher education white paper: Universities "critical" to UK's success' and only further down noted 'And a new arts and humanities research council will be set up.'[1] Similarly, *The Times* led with 'Clarke tackles research and the social divide' though it eventually managed to slip in that 'An arts and humanities research council will be established by 2005.'[2]

This journalistic attention was not misdirected. By 31 January *The Times Higher* was reporting that 170 MPs including 130 Labour backbenchers had signed an anti-top up petition.[3] The same issue of *THES* reported that Diana Warwick, chief executive of Universities UK, had taken the floor of the House of Lords to warn against the concentration of research funding signalled in the higher education paper.[4] An earlier *THES* headline had proclaimed that 'cash is [to be] lavished on RAE giants' and an editorial grumbled that Cardinal Newman 'would not have recognized the government's concept of glorified further education colleges with a sideline in helping local business.'[5] Nonetheless, the weekly did note that the White Paper 'recognizes the social and cultural benefits from arts research' in calling for the prompt establishment of an Arts and Humanities Research Council. And Warwick was also quoted as 'Welcoming the government's commitment to establishing an Arts and Humanities Research Council'.[6]

The warm welcome accorded to the proposal for an AHRC evinced assiduous, behind-the-scenes work by its supporters. On the very day the White Paper was announced, the Scottish Executive issued a press release. It noted Scotland's role in funding the AHRB and observed that changing to an AHRC would require legislation in both the Scottish and the UK Parliaments. But the central and encouraging message came in a quotation from Iain Gray, Scotland's Minister for Enterprise and Lifelong Learning:

> Following wide consultation with the sector in Scotland, the Scottish Executive is delighted to support the creation of a new AHRC. ... I look forward to working closely with the other administrations to ensure as speedy an introduction as possible.[7]

Similar support came several months later in the RCUK's response to the White Paper. 'We particularly welcome the proposal to create an Arts and Humanities Research Council and agree that it is very important to place the organization of the arts and humanities on the same footing as the funding for science, engineering and technology.' The RCUK did challenge the White Paper's fascination with the concentration of research. It reminded the Government that the Research Councils 'fund excellence wherever it is found' and stressed that direct funding to institutions 'should as far as possible follow the research and not pre-empt where it will go.' The RCUK even insisted with respect to its prospective new partner (as well as the social sciences) that there was little evidence that further concentration of research in the arts and humanities 'would be useful' and that implementing it 'would be particularly problematical.'[8] The AHRB's own response to the White Paper made much the same points.[9]

That the proposal to establish an AHRC was finding a wide welcome was confirmed in the House of Commons. Conservative MP Timothy Boswell had been Parliamentary Under-Secretary of State for the Department for Education from 1992 to 1995. On 18 March 2003 he concluded his discussion of the White Paper 'by paying the Minister a compliment. I am delighted that the long process of establishing an Arts and Humanities Research Council has reached fruition. Such processes always take a long time. This one started about 10 years ago, but we have got there.'[10]

Perhaps it is even more revealing when politicians begin to appropriate not just the credit for some measure, but the arguments for it. A few weeks later, on 3 April, two Labour members were discussing the school curriculum. MP David Chaytor was arguing against the unproductive separation of science from the arts and humanities that, he thought, led to 'a switching-off from the study of science at an early age'. His colleague, Tony McWalter, interjected that the Government had just agreed to an AHRC and that 'the chief executive of that fledgling research council now attends meetings of the other research councils.' McWalter went on that heads of other Research Councils had initially wondered, 'What are these people doing here, and what use will we get out of it?' Later, however, 'they asked how they could ever have done without them.' McWalter noted that the research councils were 'finding all sorts of connections and synergies.' While reminding his colleague that their discussion was about schools, not universities, Mr. Chaytor allowed 'My hon. Friend makes an extremely important point, and it is good to see that sort of progressive development in higher education.'[11]

Later in the spring of 2003 Charles Clarke himself was locked in discussion of the White Paper with the Commons Select Committee on Education and Skills. He was 'glad' that the then-Conservative MP Robert Jackson had 'applauded what we are doing on the Arts and Humanities Research Council. I think that is important.' Clarke then tried to build on this point of agreement to make 'the case for collaboration across the range more profoundly'.[12]

By mid-summer such intimations of widespread support for an AHRC were confirmed in the *Commentary on Responses Received* published by the Department of Education and Skills. It reported receiving 719 responses to the entire White Paper, including 93 from institutions of higher education, 92 from parents, and 78 from education organizations, 58 from student groups, and 56 from individual students. The summary began with the good news: 'Proposals that were particularly welcomed included the formation of the Arts and Humanities Research Council, the development of Knowledge Exchanges, Centres of Excellence for Teaching, the development of foundation degrees and the abolition of up-front tuition fees.'[13] The summary then acknowledged two significant areas of concern to the respondents: that universities might be separated into teaching and research institutions; and that students could be faced with discouraging levels of debt. Without backing away from its core proposals, the Government denied any 'intention of simply removing all [research] funding from departments outside the very best'. It did not, however, acknowledge any difference between concentration resulting from competitive review of research proposals and concentration as a prior and explicit purpose of funding policy.[14] Moreover, the Government's response actively defended variable fees based on 'the differing characteristics of the courses and subjects' without considering any possible impact of the variations on the subject areas themselves.[15] However, on at least one topic—research in the arts and humanities—the Government was eager to associate itself with what it was hearing. 'We welcome support for our proposals and intend to bring forward legislation to create the AHRC as soon as practicable.'[16]

By the Labour Party Conference at the end of September 2003 the Government knew they were headed for a showdown, particularly over the fees issue. Their determination to play their cards well became nearly palpable. The Queen's speech opening Parliament on 26 November began by heralding a bill 'to enable more young people to benefit from higher education. ... Universities will be placed on a sound financial footing.'[17] When Charles Clarke rose on 8 January 2004 to introduce the Higher Education Bill, he first announced major concessions to enhance support for low income students. A headline in *The Times Higher* commented 'Blair Bets All on Wooing Rebels'.[18]

The bill itself took a well-considered if surprising shape. In 1997 the Dearing Report had recommended an Arts and Humanities Research Council on page 176 of its more than 460 pages. In 2003 the Higher Education White Paper recommended an AHRC on page 32 of its 106 pages. A year later the order of presentation had changed noticeably. In the words of the official Hansard record: 'Mr. Secretary Clarke presented a Bill to make provision about research in the arts and humanities and...'[19] Part One of the Higher Education Bill was devoted to 'Research in Arts and Humanities.' Its ten sections began: '1. Arts and Humanities Research Council'.

The next day Geoffrey Crossick, Chief Executive of the AHRB, observed in *The Times Higher* that 'So much controversy has swirled around the higher education bill that it may come as a surprise to discover that at least a part of it has commanded virtually unanimous support.'[20] On the same day the AHRB issued a press release with the headline: 'HE Bill creates new research council for arts and humanities.' Allowing that the bill had already generated heated debate, the press release emphasized that one proposal had 'garnered all-party and public support.' The evolution of the AHRB into an AHRC, it confidently asserted, 'is uncontested and supported throughout the UK.'[21] Once marginal to the higher education debate, the Research Council proposal was beginning to seem like a modest advantage in, as well as a potential casualty of, the showdown.

Crossick's essay explained how the AHRB had rapidly established itself as indispensable, making possible new ways of doing research. It saw research in the arts and humanities as feeding into economic and social wellbeing, even though its 'fundamental importance' was in providing ways to understand our world that could enrich humanity. Crossick concluded, 'Although this aspect of the higher education bill may have had little press attention, it is of great significance.'[22]

The climax of the political storm came quickly. On 27 January 2004, just after 12:40 pm, Charles Clarke introduced the Commons' second reading of the Higher Education Bill. He began with 'some aspects of the Bill that have received less attention but are nevertheless important. The Bill will create an arts and humanities research council—the first new research council since 1994 and a major step forward for the arts and humanities community, giving those disciplines their proper status.'[23] The ensuing debate went on for nearly seven hours, but almost none of it concerned the proposal for an arts and humanities research council. About two o'clock Liberal Democrat Phil Willis did note, 'we support the establishment of an arts and humanities council that will raise the profile of both in higher education.'[24] Four hours later the self-identified last Back-Bench speaker, Conservative Tim Boswell, sounded 'a note of minor agreement' finding the provisions for an AHRC 'acceptable'.[25]

Another Conservative, John Bercow, raised the only substantive question: given the importance of the UK research base, why were the first ten articles 'silent about the wider pursuit of necessary commercial sponsorship?' His colleague Tim Yeo, Shadow Secretary of State for Public Services, Health and Education, put this 'important point' off to committee proceedings.[26] Toward the end of the day, Labour MP Gordon Marsden tried to calm the general storm by reminding the House 'the Bill is not just about variable fees. We must consider the whole package—the arts and humanities research council, an independent negotiator and the Office for Fair Access. All those will be lost if the Bill is voted down tonight.'[27] At 6:59 pm the Higher Education Bill was voted up at its Second Reading: 316 ayes to 311 noes.[28] The next day *The Yorkshire Post* summed up the drama as: 'Disappointment as Blair escapes getting duffed up by his own side.'[29]

NOTES

[1] *The Guardian* (London) 23 January 2003, Guardian Home Pages p. 11.

[2] *The Times* (London) 23 January 2003, Home News p. 4.

[3] THES 31 January 2003.

[4] THES 31 January 2003.

[5] THES 23 January 2003.

[6] THES 23 January 2003.

[7] Scottish Executive, 'News Release: Change in status for arts and humanities' 22 January 2003.

[8] 'RCUK Response to the White Paper on the Future of Higher Education', Annex A of *AHRB Response to the White Paper on the Future of Higher Education*, pp. 3-4.

[9] *AHRB Response to the White Paper on the Future of Higher Education*, p. 1. In its response the AHRB 'very much welcomes the decision of the Government and the devolved administrations' to establish a full research council providing research in the arts and humanities access to same sources of funding and making integration with work of other disciplines easier. It notes that AHRB funding is selective 'but interestingly not by design as we currently operate entirely in the responsive mode.' It points out that the creative and performing arts have more strength in the non research-intensive higher education institutions than would be the case in other disciplines, including the humanities, and urges that any policy of research concentration should not weaken that strength.

[10] *Commons Hansard* 18 Mar 2003: Column 220WH. Cf. Chapter I, p. 4. While a Minister, Boswell had actually conveyed to the British Academy the Government's decision in 1993 *not* to establish a Humanities Research Council. Peter Brown, personal communication, 5 October 2007.

[11] *Commons Hansard* 3 April 2003: Column 347WH.

[12] *Commons Select Committee Report* 23 June 2003.

[13] Department for Education and Skills, *Commentary on White Paper Responses Received* [no date] p.1. [hereafter 'Commentary']

[14] Commentary p. 5.

[15] Commentary p. 16.

[16] Commentary p. 4.

[17] 'Text: the Queen's speech', *Guardian Unlimited* Wednesday 26 November 2003.

[18] THES 9 January 2004 p. 2.

[19] *Commons Hansard* 8 January 2004: Column 441 'BILL PRESENTED: Higher Education'.

[20] THES 9 January 2004.

[21] AHRB News & Press Release 9 January 2004.

[22] THES 9 January 2004.

[23] *Commons Hansard* 27 January 2004: Column 167.

[24] *Commons Hansard* 27 January 2004: Column 196.

[25] *Commons Hansard* 27 January 2004: Column 260.

[26] *Commons Hansard* 27 January 2004: Column 188.

[27] *Commons Hansard* 27 January 2004: Column 259.

[28] *Commons Hansard* 27 January 2004: Column 270.

[29] *Yorkshire Post*, 28 January 2004, p. 4.

X

Deliberations and Predispositions

Writing later about the progress of the Higher Education Bill toward the statute books, *The Times Higher* commented about this drama of 27 January 2004: 'The rebels had gambled all on this showdown and, when the vote failed, the threat they posed largely melted away.'[1] Thereafter each stage of considering the Higher Education Bill seemed also to add definition and reality to the Arts and Humanities Research Council. Clearing its Second Reading meant that the Higher Education Bill could go to a committee of the House of Commons for more detailed review. Between 10 February and 9 March there were fifteen sittings of Standing Committee H to examine the proposed legislation clause by clause. Since the Bill's first part concerned Research in Arts and Humanities, that part was considered first, in morning and afternoon sessions on 10 February. Alan Johnson, Minister for Lifelong Learning, Further and Higher Education, had very effectively taken up the lead on the Bill for the Government. At one point Johnson commented that, to his knowledge, there had been no demonstrations against the arts and humanities aspect of the Bill[2] and at another point that he believed that it had unanimous support.[3] Other members of the committee were quick to aver that they needed time to give every aspect of the bill careful scrutiny.

In actual point of fact, however, the first issue to be raised was the question from Conservative Tim Collins as to whether, given its proposed location in the Department of Trade and Industry, 'The research council will have an opportunity to thrive.'[4] Johnson gave the expected assurances, adding that this location also would provide the link to commerce that had been of interest in the 27 January floor debate.[5] Discussion proceeded in a genial tone, with members offering 'probing amendments' to elicit such assurances as that

AHRB employee rights would transfer to the new AHRC. One amendment, offered by a Welsh Plaid Cymru MP, was virtually the inverse of the Government's preoccupation with concentrating research. It would have reserved ('bottom-sliced') ten per cent of funding in each of the Research Councils for those institutions that 'benefited the least from the distribution of the other ninety per cent'.[6] Conservative Chris Grayling quickly responded that establishing the AHRC was itself the appropriate sort of 'counterbalance' to predetermined concentration. He argued that the amendment would take away the ability of the Research Councils to channel funding to the best and most effective projects. He added 'The peer review system that says—regardless of the institution or where it is situated in the country—that funding for a research project will be provided based on merit, on the assessment of peers and their judgment of the quality of the work, has to be the right way to go.'[7]

Regional concerns were prominent in the committee's deliberations on 10 February, partly because of vote counting against the Bill's Third Reading, partly because the Government's Bill introduced a new approach to the matter. Among other steps intended to appeal to the devolved areas, *The Review of Arts and Humanities Research Funding* had suggested that the AHRC charter 'should explicitly include a duty to promote research into cultural aspects of the various parts of the UK.' But clause 10 of the Higher Education Bill took a more dramatic approach. Over and above the creation of the AHRC, it empowered the Welsh, Scottish, and Northern Irish administrations to support arts and humanities research with respect to their own region. Chris Grayling launched a series of amendments to strip away this aspect of the Bill. Don Touhig, Parliamentary Under-Secretary of State for Wales, took up defence of the Government's position. He argued that the devolved administrations already had the same authority to complement the work of established science and technology research councils. Touhig also pointed out that, with respect to the proposed AHRC, 'Those powers are among the key mechanisms by which we are implementing the review of arts and humanities research funding.'[8] Ultimately Grayling seemed to still his apparent anxieties about over-regulation and multiplying bureaucratic entities. Clause 10 stood as read.

After the 10 February Committee sessions the prospect of an AHRC became increasingly real. Indicative was the position of the National Postgraduate Committee. On 19 March *The Times Higher* reported the Committee's warning that tuition fees would hinder students from continuing their education. Consequently, 'NPC will oppose the [Higher Education] bill because of variable fees although it supports plans for an Arts and Humanities Research Council...'[9] Across many points of view it was reassuring that the prospective AHRC was to be built on a known and reliable foundation: the AHRB. At one point Charles Clarke was asked what the AHRC's disciplinary remit would be, the sort of question normally fraught with contention. But Clarke found ready to hand a calming and economical response: the remit would be the same as that of the AHRB.[10]

Already on 1 March Chris Henshall, Director of the DTI/OST Science and Engineering Base Group, had written to both Brian Follett and Geoffrey Crossick to report 'the outcome of our consultation with Ministers on appointments to the new Council'. While firm commitments couldn't yet be made, 'Ministers are presently minded' to appoint Follett as first Chair of the Council, Crossick as first Chief Executive and Deputy Chair, and other members of the Council's Management Board as their terms would have stood with the AHRB. Also, the Ministers were content with a proposed template for the membership of the AHRC Council showing eight academic members and five non-academic members from government, business, and the public sector.[11]

On 26 March *The Times Higher* even reported that, while Crossick welcomed what was 'the least controversial aspect of the higher education bill'—the provision to turn AHRB into 'a fully fledged research council'—he was now worried that, if the new Council were to succeed, serious funding inequalities would have to be addressed.[12] On 31 March 2004 the House of Commons met for the Third Reading of the Higher Education Bill. Research in the arts and humanities was not discussed. The bill passed: ayes 309, noes 248.

*

On the very next day, 1 April 2004, the Higher Education Bill was introduced into the House of Lords. The proposal for an Arts and Humanities Research Council was received warmly on all sides. The House resolved itself into a committee to discuss the bill on 10, 13, 18 and 25 May, with discussion of Part 1 that had to do with arts and humanities research coming on the first day. The Conservative Lord Renfrew, an eminent archaeologist, opened up discussion of two fundamental academic issues. He pointed out that AHRB had not accepted applications from overseas British research institutions and sought assurances that AHRC would reverse this policy. Baroness Ashton, principal Labour manager for the bill, made Renfrew 'a happy Peer' by explaining that once the AHRC was funded through the Office of Science and Technology, it would no longer be restricted to funding only universities. Born in the Higher Education Funding Councils, the AHRB was an agency for funding arts and humanities research in universities. The remit of the AHRC could be much more comprehensive.

Renfrew also provoked much discussion by trying to attach an 'Academic Salaries Review Board' to the AHRC section of the bill. Many Lords lamented the state of academic salaries, and found it unlikely that the prospective increase in university revenues would go for this purpose. Eventually Renfrew withdrew the amendment as misplaced in the arts and humanities part of the legislation. On 8 June, however, as Lords was preparing its report on the Higher Education Bill, Renfrew revived the proposal, announcing his intention 'to test the opinion of the House. It is an occasion to stand up and be counted.' Fifty-seven Lords were content with the proposal for an Academic Salaries Review Board; one hundred and twenty-two were not.[13]

Also on 10 May Baroness Sharp, a Liberal Democrat and well-know economist, proposed an amendment that probed the intended governance relationship between the Department of Trade and Industry and the AHRC. Baroness Warwick, chief executive of Universities UK, averred that the bill had got 'the right balance' between 'the legitimate influence' of the Government minister in directing the way in which public money should be spent and the proposed council's freedom of operation.[14] Baroness Ashton detailed that 'right balance' by outlining how Research Councils function: 'receipt of their grant, strategic overview, reporting, because this is public money, but with autonomy over whom they choose to support'.[15] The distinguished neurologist, Lord Walton, did not object to these arrangements, but did note that much had changed in the twenty-six years since his service on the Medical Research Council. 'In those days we would not have accepted [the clause] relating to a direction by the Secretary of State because independence was one of the principles underlying the activities of the research councils.'[16] Baroness Sharp accepted that ministerial directives could be appropriate, but insisted that they should be transparent. 'It is better that the situation come out in the open and there is an explicit letter of direction, as distinct from the Minister simply putting pressure on the research council chief executive and compliance behind the scenes.'[17]

Having made her point, Baroness Sharp withdrew the proposed amendment, but her exposition of academic governance did reveal that separate, if complementary, principles of legitimacy were at work in the deliberations leading to an AHRC. She had explained the second principle during the 19 April Second Reading of the Higher Education Bill. She insisted that 'peer review which grades according to perceived academic excellence, effectively replaces the market in much of academia and has its own rewards in terms of status and promotion.' Thus her party objected 'to the "marketization" of knowledge' that encourages students to choose subjects on the basis of costs and monetary rewards. She cited the American Robert Reich's warning against giving up the public vision of higher education, allowing it to become a private good.[18]

As in the House of Commons, the most serious opposition to Part 1 of the Higher Education Bill in the House of Lords had to do with clause ten which enabled the devolved administrations to provide for arts and humanities research on their own. Given that an AHRC for the entire UK was authorized in clause one, clause ten could be seen as unnecessary duplication and overlap. The Conservative Baroness Seccombe objected to what she called an unfunded 'proliferation of quangos'.[19] Lord Walton pointed out, however, that the devolved administrations were already able to undertake a variety of scientific research even though this might overlap with the remits of the existing UK Research Councils.

> Similarly, the new research council will have a UK-wide role and each of the devolved administrations may, if they wish, promote research in the field of humanities and so on, which may, for instance, be relevant to the culture and history of Scotland, Wales and Northern Ireland. Surely, that is a comparable situation to that which exists in the other research councils and is framed in exactly the same way.

Baroness Ashton commended Lord Walton's position and also noted 'the critical relevance of having flexibility within the devolved administrations, who [sic] are very supportive of this part of the

Bill.'[20] The Opposition's leading spokesman, Lord Forsyth, may have already made a similar point—in a much more acid way—at the Bill's Second Reading on 19 April: the Bill was 'the product of a political fix between the Government and their revolting Back-Benchers and universities desperate for cash' and the Government had got 'the Bill through the Commons using the votes of Scottish MPs'.[21]

In general, discussion of the Higher Education Bill in the House of Lords was thoughtful and deliberative. It had one notable success: an amendment delaying the imposition of higher university fees for those students who took 'a gap year' in 2004-2005. But by the end of June the House had completed the work it felt it could do. A press release from the AHRB reported that on the evening of 1 July 2004 the Higher Education Bill received Royal Assent. 'It is now the Higher Education Act.'[22] Part 1, Clause 1 of the Act defines 'the Arts and Humanities Research Council' as:

> a body to be established by Royal Charter wholly or mainly for objects consisting of, or comprised in, the following—
> (a) carrying out, facilitating, encouraging and supporting—
>> (i) research in the arts and humanities, and
>> (ii) instruction in the arts and humanities,
> (b) advancing and disseminating knowledge in, and promoting understanding of, the arts and humanities,
> (c) promoting awareness of the body's activities, and
> (d) providing advice on matters relating to the body's activities.

Clauses 2 through 9 dealt with the transfer of AHRB property, paying expenses incurred by the AHRC, rendering accounts, and so on. The familiar Clause 10 extended powers for research in the arts and humanities to the authorities for Wales, Scotland, and Northern Ireland.[23]

In a 2 July 2004 press release the AHRB celebrated that 'the creation of an Arts and Humanities Research Council (AHRC) in April 2005 moved a step closer as the Higher Education Bill received the Royal Assent last night. It is now the Higher Education Act.'[24] In *The Times Higher* of 6 August, Howard Newby, then head of the Higher Education Funding Council of England, surveyed his new challenges under the Act, taking a few sentences to see off an old responsibility. He celebrated 'achievement' of the AHRC, 'one that Hefce has helped bring about.'[25] But at the AHRB itself, Crossick remained alert that 'there is further intensive work to be done ... the next stage of the process ... requires approval of the Scottish Parliament.'[26]

*

In fact, work with the Scottish Parliament had been going on in parallel with the progress of the Higher Education Bill at Westminster. It centred on a 'Sewel motion', a parliamentary device to allow the UK Parliament to consider a matter that had been devolved to Scotland. Simultaneous with the dramatic Second Reading of the Bill in the UK Parliament on 27 January 2004, such a 'Sewel motion' was considered by the Enterprise and Culture Committee of the Scottish Parliament. The problem (as suggested in Chapter VII above) was that, since the AHRC was being created after the Scotland Act 1998, its function could not have been reserved to the UK as had the functions of the other Research Councils. Moreover, approximately £5.4 million, Scotland's anticipated share of AHRB financing for 2005-2006 had already been committed to the Scottish Higher Education Funding Council. If the AHRC were to come into being as anticipated on 1 April 2005, the beginning of the fiscal year, those funds would have to be transferred back to Westminster, an unnatural act for any politician.

The very Clause 10 that had come under such fire in the UK Parliament provided a powerful argument to Deputy Minister Jim Wallace addressing the Scottish Enterprise and Culture Committee. Not only would the Charter of the AHRC provide for culturally specific research, but the Higher Education Bill also 'made provision for direct funding of arts and humanities research by the Scottish Executive.'[27] The same argument had been featured in the 'Sewel Memorandum' prepared by the Scottish Executive to accompany the motion.[28] Wallace could also reassure the Committee that 'the Scottish academic community, after wide consultation strongly supports proposals to establish an arts and humanities research council. This includes academics with specific Scottish interests...'[29] The accompanying memorandum suggested why Scottish academics might come to this conclusion. Keeping Scotland out of the AHRC 'was seen as likely to be deeply damaging to the sector, through loss of competitive status of Scottish research in UK terms.'[30] Both the memorandum and Wallace's presentation had a good deal of data to show that Scotland had done very well by the AHRB, and the memo managed to insinuate that funding for arts and humanities research could 'benefit from being part of the same system of budgets set by the DTI for the Science Research Councils.'[31] When asked if the Department of Trade and Industry had expertise in arts and humanities research, Wallace suggested that 'the differences in methodology and approach between science and the arts are narrowing,'[32] an attractive prospect in light of the memorandum's report that 'artificial boundaries between the different sectors ... are reducing the opportunities for innovation.'[33]

The Sewel motion went to the floor of the Scottish Parliament on 12 February 2004. Again Wallace could cite Clause 10 as well as argue from Scotland's experience with the AHRB. 'We certainly punch above our weight and there is no reason to think that we will not do that after the arts and humanities research council is established. Not being part of the council could be damaging to arts and humanities research in Scotland.'[34] The Scottish Parliament passed the Sewel motion by a vote of 77 for, 22 against, 10 abstentions. Twenty-one of the twenty-two votes against came from members of the Scottish National Party, one of whose spokesmen had opposed the motion 'on the usual ground that Sewel motions are inappropriate'.[35]

Once the Higher Education Act received Royal Assent on 1 July 2004, the Scottish Parliament, as well as UK Houses of Commons and Lords, had to enact the order making the work of the AHRC (though not all research in the arts and humanities) a matter reserved to the UK. On 16 December 2004 *The Scotland Act 1998 (Modifications of Schedule 5) Order 2004* recorded that it had been laid before and approved by a resolution in each of the three bodies.[36] Also on 16 December 2004 a warrant was issued for a Royal Charter for 'one body corporate under the name "The Arts and Humanities Research Council"'.[37] As if to confirm the close political calculations by which this momentous result was achieved, barely a month later the Scottish Executive issued a similar order commencing section 10(3) of the Higher Education Act by which it too could provide for arts and humanities research.[38]

NOTES

[1] THES 9 July 2004.
[2] *Commons Select Committee* 10 February 2004 Column 4.
[3] *Commons Select Committee* 10 February 2004 Column 17.
[4] *Commons Select Committee* 10 February 2004 Column 11.
[5] *Commons Select Committee* 10 February 2004 Column 17.
[6] *Commons Select Committee* 10 February 2004 Column 22.
[7] *Commons Select Committee* 10 February 2004 Column 27.
[8] *Commons Select Committee* 10 February 2004 Column 70.
[9] THES 19 March 2004; cf. THES 13 August 2004.
[10] *House of Commons Hansard Written Answers* for 23 February 2004 pt. 46.

[11] Dr Chris Henshall to Brian Follett 1 March 2004; Dr Chris Henshall to Professor Geoffrey Crossick 1 March 2004.

[12] THES 26 March 2004.

[13] Overseas British research institutes and schools have been supported through the British Academy since 1950, a relationship unaltered by the establishment of the AHRB. *BA Some Documents*, p. 24. *Lords Hansard* 8 June 2004 Column 172.

[14] *Lords Hansard* 10 May 2004 Column 18.

[15] *Lords Hansard* 10 May 2004 Column 22.

[16] *Lords Hansard* 10 May 2004 Column 20.

[17] *Lords Hansard* 10 May 2004 Column 25.

[18] *Lords Hansard* 19 April 2004 Column 24.

[19] *Lords Hansard* 10 May 2004 Columns 64-65, 71. Quangos: quasi-autonomous non-governmental organizations.

[20] *Lords Hansard* 10 May 2004 Columns 70-71.

[21] *Lords Hansard* 19 Apr 2004 Column 20.

[22] AHRB News and Press Releases 2 July 2004.

[23] *Higher Education Act* 2004.

[24] AHRB News and Press Releases 2 July 2004.

[25] THES 6 August 2004 p. 12.

[26] AHRB News and Press Releases 2 July 2004.

[27] *Meeting Number 4 Official Report Enterprise and Culture Committee* Scottish Parliament 27 January 2004 Columns 504, 505.

[28] Scottish Executive, *Sewel Memorandum* paragraphs 15, 16.

[29] *Meeting Number 4 Official Report Enterprise and Culture Committee* Scottish Parliament 27 January 2004 Column 505.

[30] Scottish Executive, *Sewel Memorandum* paragraph 8. Like other Scottish support for the proposed AHRC, this praiseworthy statement of academic principle—and reality—owed much to such academic leaders as Stewart Sutherland, Principal and Vice-Chancellor of the University of Edinburgh (through 2002), John Caughie, Dean of the Faculty of Arts, University of Glasgow, and their colleagues. Michael Jubb of the AHRB did much to marshal this support in Scotland.

[31] Scottish Executive, *Sewel Memorandum* paragraph 6.

[32] *Meeting Number 4 Official Report Enterprise and Culture Committee* Scottish Parliament 27 January 2004 Column 506.

[33] Scottish Executive, *Sewel Memorandum* paragraph 7.

[34] Scottish Parliament 12 February 2004 Column 5909.

[35] Scottish Parliament 12 February 2004 Columns 5914-5916, 5908.

[36] *The Scotland Act 1998 (Modifications of Schedule 5) Order 2004.*

[37] *Royal Charter* (Draft) 16 December 2004.

[38] *The Higher Education Act 2004 (Commencement No. 1) (Scotland) Order 2005.* The Royal Charter, of course, did include the provision that the Council 'advance knowledge and understanding … relating to cultural aspects of the different parts of Our United Kingdom.'

XI

Board to Council

The Arts and Humanities Research Board approached its 2005 transformation having built up an impressive array of assets. Its £83.6 million budget for that year was nearly one-fifth larger than that of the National Endowment for the Humanities in the United States, whose population was five times as large.[1] The AHRB was explicitly included in the UK's *Science and Innovation Investment Framework 2004-2014* which foresaw UK investment in research rising from 1.9% to 2.5% of national income over the ten years and the budget of the AHRC's parent OST rising from £2.913 billion in 2005-06 to £3.828 billion in 2007-08.[2]

The core responsibility of the Arts and Humanities Research Council would be the work of approximately 12,000 active arts and humanities researchers in the UK. Since 1998 the AHRB had made over 4000 awards involving more than 5000 researchers.[3] Two hundred and forty different individuals had already served on its committees, panels, and other forms of peer review. By October 2004, 456 scholars had become the first members of the AHRB's College of Peer Reviewers and by the end of the AHRC's first year another 133 members would be added. Countless others had participated in the AHRB's consultations and workshops. In addition, the AHRC would inherit a seasoned yet lively staff of 88 full-time members.[4] Across the UK, in the institutions of government and of the academy, many had been engaged with the AHRB and were actively committed to its fulfilment as a Research Council.

Transformation into the Arts and Humanities Research Council involved a number of administrative matters that required careful attention before April 1, 2005. The transition out of charitable status and the transfer of the AHRB's assets and obligations to a new Non-

Departmental Public Body (NDPD) turned out to require even more subtle manoeuvring than winning charitable status in the first place. Moving into the Office of Science and Technology and thus the Department of Trade and Industry meant a new administrative regime and more emphasis on actually demonstrating that the research supported by the AHRC was valuable, sustainable, and of comparative international strength.[5] It also meant, though, that the Council would be able to plan on the basis of multi-year funding and that it would be expected not only to respond to ideas from the field but also to undertake significant strategic initiatives. Indeed, the first of the objects to which the Royal Charter dedicated the AHRC was 'to promote and support by any means high-quality basic, *strategic* and applied research and related post-graduate training in the arts and humanities' [*emphasis added*].[6]

In the summer of 2004 the AHRB had already adopted a new strategic plan that committed the organization 'to develop and to implement strategic initiatives to support research in areas of intellectual urgency'.[7] Whether this formulation referred primarily to potential intellectual breakthroughs or to social emergencies was left indeterminate. The first Strategic Programmes launched were 'Diasporas, Migrations and Identities' and 'Landscape and Environment'.[8] In any case, the AHRB noted that 85% of its 2004-05 funding was in the responsive mode, supporting 'the engine room for new ideas'.[9]

Greater sensitivity to strategic concerns did seem to spread throughout the organization. To get control of the very large commitment of funds to the Research Centres (cf. Chapter VI), 'Phase 2' funding was awarded to those few Research Centres found to be working at a level of 'demonstrable national and international importance'. Of the first ten AHRC Research Centres only the one for Irish and Scottish studies and the one on the Evolution of Cultural Diversity were judged to meet this ambitious criterion.[10] In the Postgraduate Programme some awards were set aside for fields endangered because too few students were pursuing doctoral research: ancient and medieval materials and artefacts; early languages of the British Isles and their literatures; East and Central European and Balkan studies; history of architecture and the built environment; and linguistics of major European languages.[11] Collaborative Doctoral Awards were introduced to foster projects between academic departments and non-academic bodies that could provide the benefits of novel resources and materials, knowledge and expertise. Also by 2004-05 the Postgraduate Programme had been fully rationalized into fewer simple categories. Against an ultimate goal of one-half the awards being at the doctoral level, 612 doctoral awards, 348 research preparation masters awards and 572 professional preparation masters awards were made that year.[12]

As it turned out, these assets were to be deployed by a transformed leadership. In May of 2005 Geoffrey Crossick left the AHRC to become Warden of Goldsmith's College. At nearly the same time Michael Jubb departed the organization he had served since *before* its beginning. Jubb became Director of the new Research Information Network. Frances Marsden served as acting Chief Executive until September of 2005. Then the new AHRC received both a new Chief Executive, Philip Esler, and a new Director of Programmes, Tony McEnery. Professor of Linguistics and English Language at Lancaster University, McEnery brought extensive experience with the use of information and computing technologies in the study of language as well as a strong record of collaboration with industry. Vice-Principal for Research at the University of St. Andrews, Esler seemed even more a man for the moment. Born and originally educated in Australia, he had a first career there as a solicitor and barrister. But having earned an Oxford PhD on the New Testament, he left what he once called 'the real world' in 1994 to teach at St. Andrews, eventually becoming Professor of Biblical Criticism. Here is how Esler once analysed Paul's *Letter to the Romans*: 'Paul is writing to groups of Judean or Greek followers of Christ in

Rome, who were locked in a conflict, largely of an ethnic nature, and he is trying to bring them together into a new common identity.' Esler then characterized his type of analysis as having 'direct bearing on contemporary social and political problems'.[13] In 2005 the new AHRC got a Chief Executive who saw ways that humanistic knowledge could transfer to today's 'real world'.

Former AHRB Chief Executive David Eastwood liked to characterize the course of the AHRB's experience by citing the subject of his yet-to-be-completed historical study. 'According to Robert Peel, the true policy in this country is to work with the instruments that come to hand.'[14] Working in a context of general respect for humanities research, a loosely associated group of inventive and resourceful people, many of them university leaders, had created an Arts and Humanities Research Council from instruments that had come to hand. But they had been working in a new age and they had found new instruments, responsibilities, and opportunities at hand.

Broadly speaking, the end of the twentieth century and the beginning of the twenty-first were marked by a transition in which the creation and deployment of knowledge was no longer a minority occupation but was becoming central to many societies. The creators of the AHRC could not merely copy older models. To succeed in this transitional age, they had open up some traditional assumptions about the humanities, even while respecting the current practice of arts and humanities researchers. The emerging AHRC had been set on a course of expanding—diplomatically, inclusively, but ambitiously—usual expectations for arts and humanities research. Another former AHRC Chief Executive, Geoffrey Crossick, used to urge the arts and humanities faculty that it was 'better to be in a world where things are tough but matter' than otherwise.[15]

Thus: knowledge, certainly knowledge in the arts and humanities, is of value for its own sake. Yes, but … such knowledge also can be expected to bring social and economic benefits. The two are not necessarily opposites. Thus, the AHRC charter charges it to 'advance knowledge and understanding of the arts and humanities … and thereby to contribute to economic competitiveness and effectiveness of public services and policy … and to enhance the quality of life and creative output of the nation.'[16] While it seems obvious as a general proposition that the arts and humanities generate such 'instrumental' as well as 'intrinsic' benefits, how this occurs is by no means well articulated. The staff and many allies of the AHRC—especially Yvonne Hawkins, the AHRC's adept and experienced Director of Knowledge and Evaluation—have a chance to help develop and apply this understanding. Offering incentives for researchers to devise new ways of 'transferring' knowledge generated in the arts and humanities to practical uses may help to illuminate this process, as well as to accelerate it. Vivid, instructive illustrations of how specific contributions to knowledge in the arts ands humanities lead to economic and social benefits will certainly have a place—along with profound interpretations, subtle accounts, and astonishing discoveries—in the ongoing story of the AHRC.

Again: the humanities and the arts do differ in some ways from the natural and social sciences,[17] but the ideal of *Wissenschaft* has been built into the structure of the AHRC. Its charter requires that it 'use its best endeavours to identify and pursue opportunities for mutually beneficial joint working with any one or more of the other Research Councils.'[18] The harmonization of administrative procedures is already well underway, but even that presents continuing challenges. Take the issue of appropriate 'metrics' by which to represent the results of research. In principle devising such a 'measure' should be no more difficult—and no more satisfactory— in the arts and humanities than in any other field of research. The humanities and arts, however, have yet to be thought about in these terms. The existing bibliometric tools were devised for the natural and social sciences; they focus on articles and English-language publication. Humanities and arts researchers tend to communicate by means of books and often publish, quite appropriately, in languages other than English. 'Mutually beneficial joint' operations with other fields of research will provide a chance for progress on such administrative or 'technical' issues.

Even more challenging will be the RCUK-wide commitment to innovation by means of interdisciplinary research. Situating the AHRC among the other Research Councils may have been a restoration of the humanities and the arts to the circle of serious knowledge seekers. But actually finding intersections among research fields to which the humanities and the arts can genuinely contribute is a challenge—and an opportunity—of historic proportions. Various joint initiatives and foresight exercises—as well as regular discussions among the Research Directors of the several councils—can help, but interdisciplinarity is not a generic matter. It involves a specific encounter among knowledge and methods from several disciplines that aims to yield a commonly understood—and frequently transformational—resolution. Given the departmental-ization of research, particularly in the UK, productive and successful interdisciplinary research will require creating strong incentives at the level of the RCUK to bring researchers from different disciplines together in an 'engine room for new ideas'.

Traditionally many humanities scholars like to see themselves as St. Jerome working alone in his study. But the case for the AHRC envisaged other approaches to research as well. It urged that, although humanities and arts research can certainly be labour-intensive, they might also be undercapitalized. Additional investments in equipment, assistance and collaboration could enable humanities and arts researchers to do even more impressive and valuable work. Few who have survived to work in the digital age will doubt this opportunity.[19] But taking advantage of this chance will not be automatic. Larger, longer grants can mean only installing bells and whistles (conferences and websites?) in Jerome's study. Identifying tools and techniques that actually enhance the scale and effectiveness of arts and humanities research—and sustaining those investments to fruition—will be a long-term mission for the AHRC and like-minded groups.

And so the AHRC was well prepared to engage frontier issues for arts and humanities research as the date of its official establishment—1 April 2005—approached. There was just one thing lacking: the Royal Charter supposed to come into effect that day. It had been authorized, we noted, on 16 December 2004. But production of the actual charter dragged on through January and February of 2005. The delay seems to have had to do with baking a new seal. Ultimately the Royal Charter for the Arts and Humanities Research Council was not signed and sealed until Friday, 11 March 2005, just three weeks before it was to come into force.

From a longer perspective, the time it took to create the AHRC could be attributed to the circumstance that the mould for Research Councils themselves had been broken *before* an AHRC was established. So it took a little while to sort out just what the AHRC would be. But the remarkable work of creating an Arts and Humanities Research Council has now been accomplished. New possibilities are opening up for the United Kingdom. Perhaps this new model of a Research Council for the arts and humanities will find further use elsewhere.[20]

NOTES

[1] Arts and Humanities Research Council, *Annual Report and Accounts 2005-06*, p. 57. [hereafter 'AHRC AR 2005-06']. NEH: $141 million FY 2006.

[2] HM Treasury, DTI, *Science and Innovation investment framework 2004–2014* (July, 2004), p. 9.

[3] AHRC, personal communication 5 September 2007. The exact numbers are 4288 proposals and 5009 people.

[4] AHRC, personal communication 29 August 2007. Cf. AHRB AR 04-05 p. 12 and AHRC AR 05-06 p. 11.

[5] AHRB AR 04-05 p. 6.

6 Royal Charter 2 (1) (a). This triadic description of types of research seems to be grounded in Donald E. Stokes, *Pasteur's Quadrant: Basic Science and Technological Innovation* (Washington, DC: The Brookings Institution Press, 1997).

7 AHRC [sic], *The Bright Path: The strategy for arts and humanities research in the UK 2004-2009* (undated) p. 7. Also AHRB AR 04-05 p. 12.

8 AHRB AR pp. 3, 12.

9 AHRB AR 04-05 p. 6.

10 AHRB AR 04-05 p. 8. Among the other nine centres, Phase 2 funding was subsequently awarded to those for Studies in Intellectual Property and Technology Law and for Musical Performance as Creative Practice. AHRC, *Podium*, Issue 6 (Spring 2007), p. 12.

11 AHRB AR 04-05 p. 18.

12 AHRB AR 04-05 p. 18.

13 Philip Esler: Think Big' in *The Guardian*, 18 October 2005. Esler's publications include *Conflict and Identity in Romans: The Social Setting of Paul's Letter* (2003); *The First Christians in Their Social Worlds: Social-Scientific Approaches to New Testament Interpretation* (1994); and *Community and Gospel in Luke-Acts: The Social and Political Motivations of Lucan Theology* (1987).

14 AHRB AR 01-02 p. 3.

15 Personal communication, 29 November 2005.

16 Royal Charter 2 (1) (b).

17 For a thoughtful elaboration of this matter see Arts and Humanities Research Board, *The Arts and Humanities: Understanding the Research Landscape* (November 2003).

18 Royal Charter 2 (3).

19 In 0.15 seconds the Worldwide Web yielded over 1400 images of Durer's iconic 1514 engraving *St. Jerome in his Study*. They included the following: http://www.ibiblio.org/wm/paint/auth/durer/engravings/st-jerome.jpg

20 Cf. Brian Follett on the AHRC as 'not far from being unique'. AHRB AR 04-05 p. 4.

Some principal characters

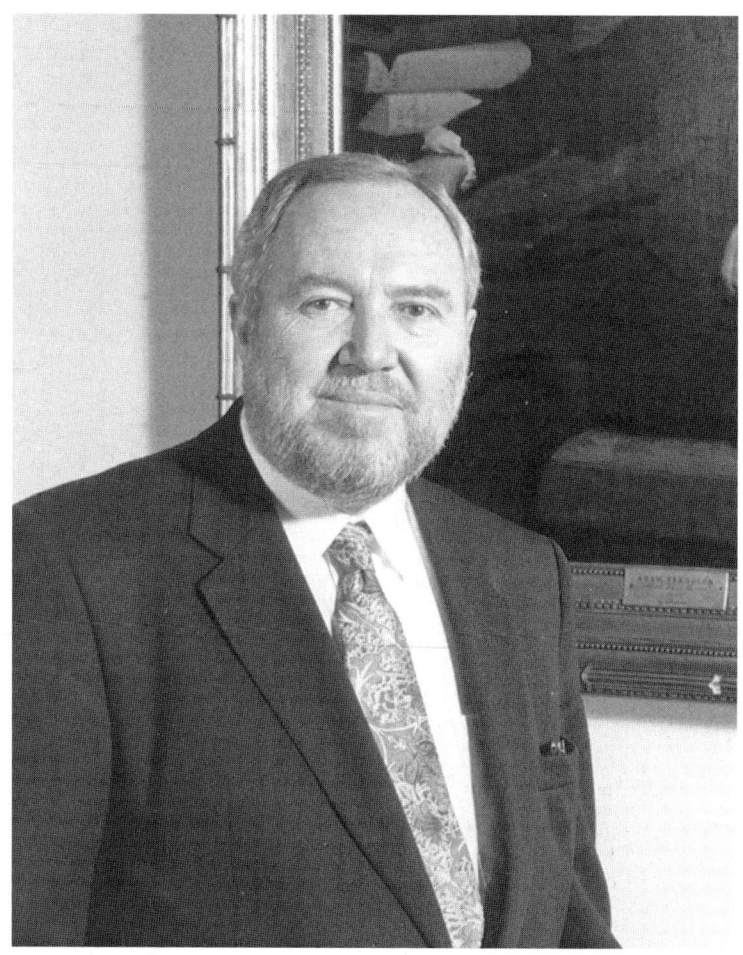

JOHN LAVER

1994–1998
Humanities Research Board
of the British Academy
Chairman

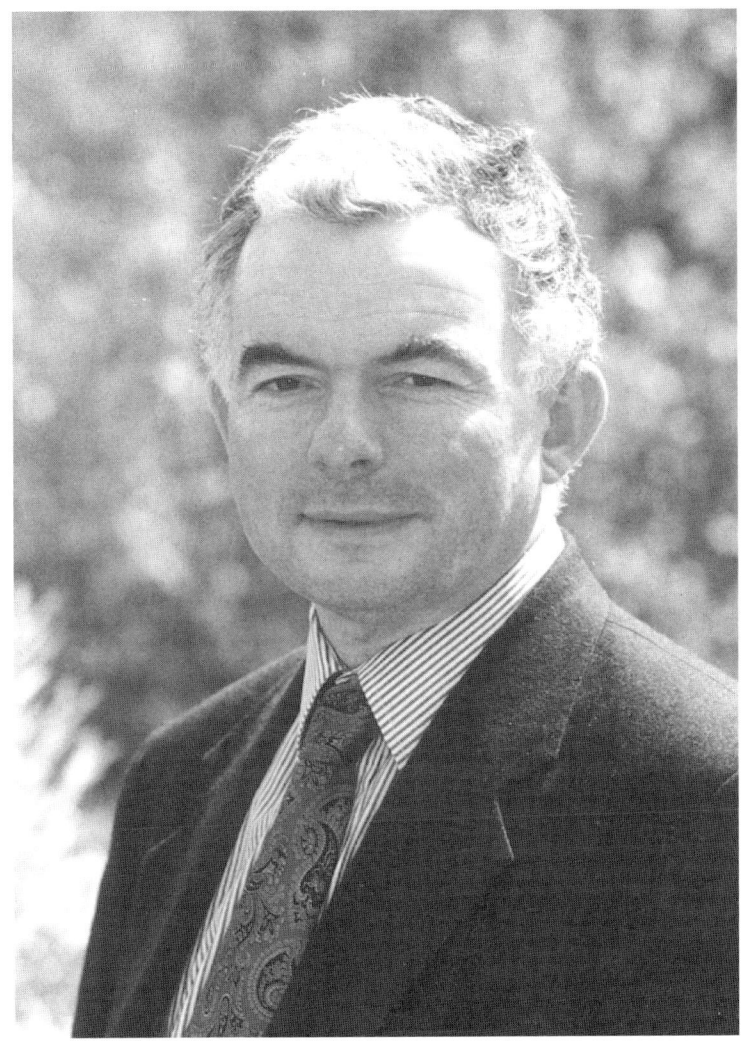

PAUL LANGFORD

1998–2000
Arts and Humanities Research Board
Chairman and Chief Executive

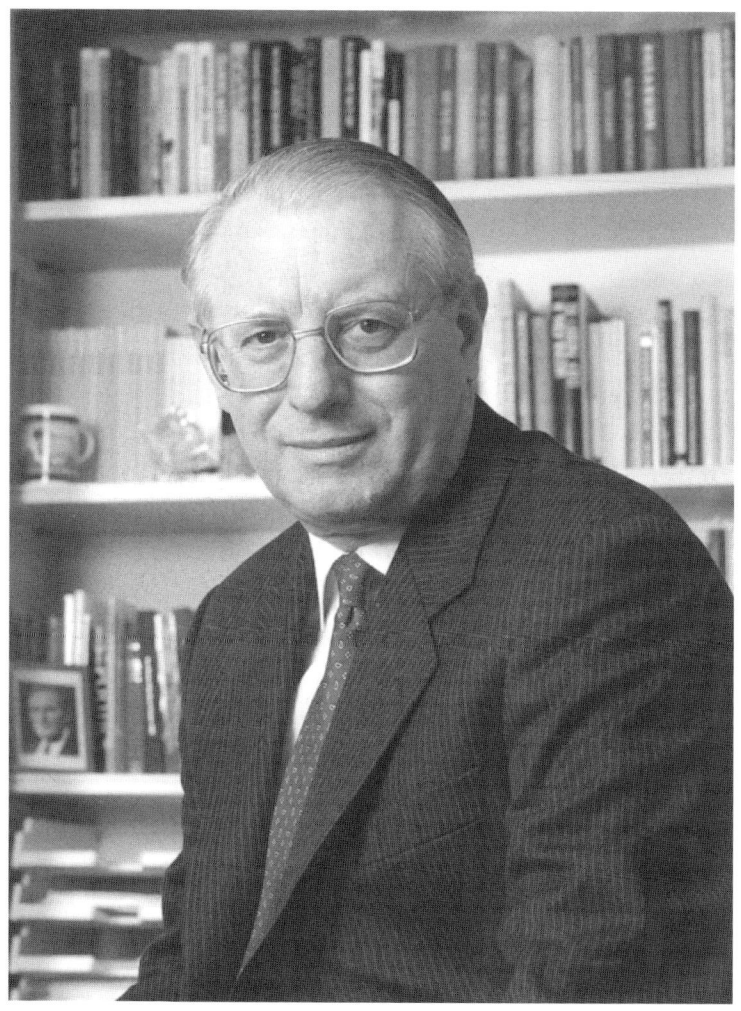

BRIAN FOLLETT

2000–2007
Arts and Humanities Research Board / Council
Chairman

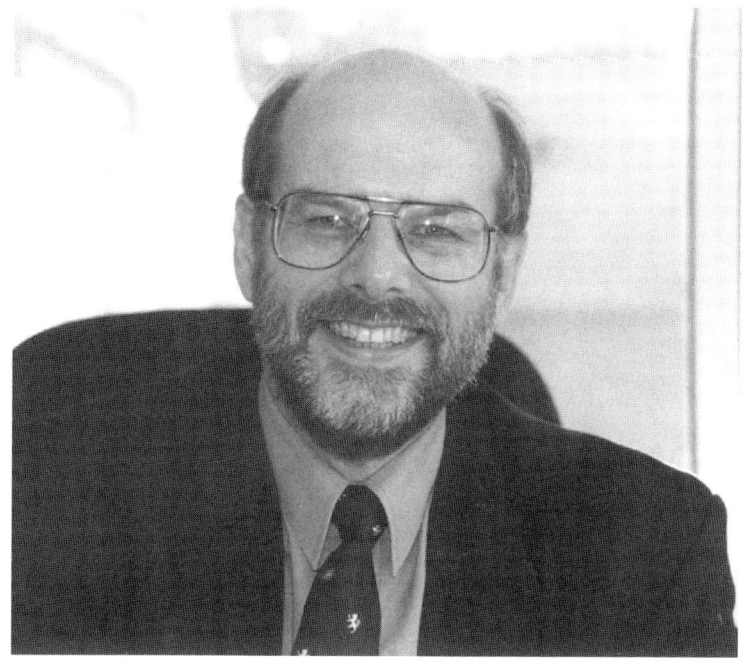

DAVID EASTWOOD

2000–2002
Arts and Humanities Research Board
Chief Executive

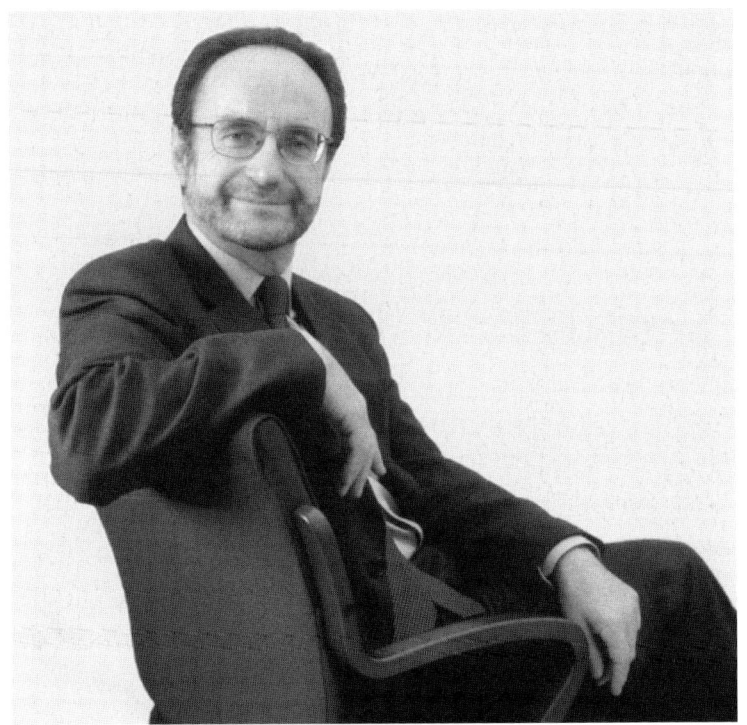

GEOFFREY CROSSICK

2002–2005
Arts and Humanities Research Board
Chief Executive

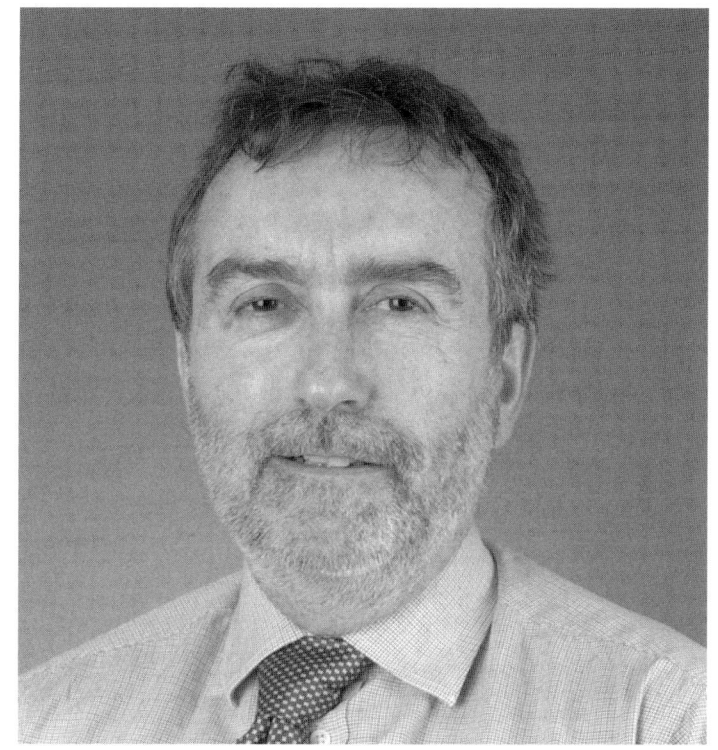

MICHAEL JUBB

1994–1998
Humanities Research Board
of the British Academy
Secretary

1998–2004
Arts and Humanities Research Board
Director of Policy & Programmes,
Deputy Chief Executive

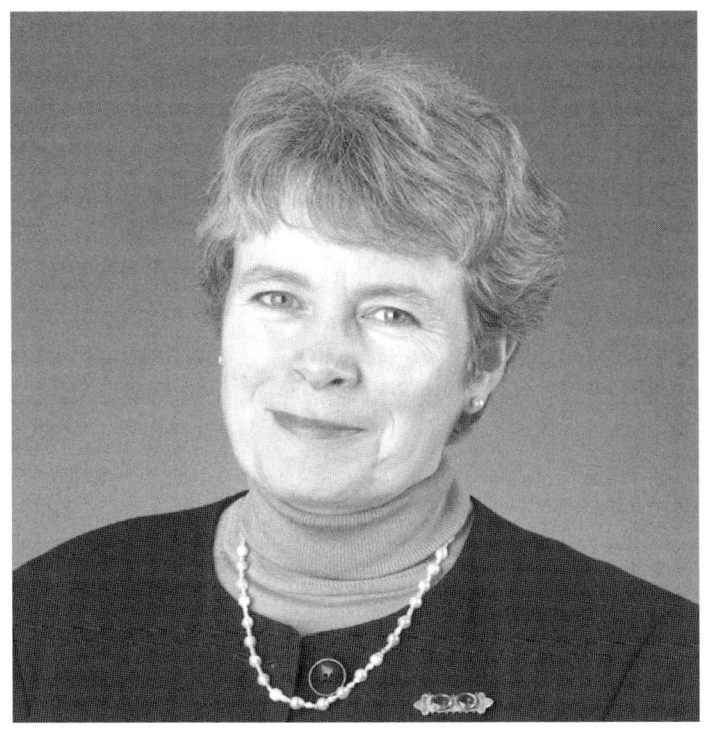

FRANCES MARSDEN

2000–2008
Arts and Humanities Research Board/Council
Director of Corporate Affairs

2005
Arts and Humanities Research Council
Interim Chief Executive